STARGAZING IN THE ATOMIC AGE

D0069314

GEORGIA REVIEW BOOKS   EDITED BY Gerald Maa

The University of Georgia Press   *Athens*

STARGAZING

IN THE

ATOMIC AGE

Essays by Anne Goldman

© 2021 by the University of Georgia Press
Athens, Georgia 30602
www.ugapress.org
All rights reserved
Designed by Erin Kirk
Set in Minion
Printed and bound by Sheridan Books
The paper in this book meets the guidelines for
permanence and durability of the Committee on
Production Guidelines for Book Longevity of the
Council on Library Resources.

Most University of Georgia Press titles are
available from popular e-book vendors.

Printed in the United States of America
24 23 22 21 20 P 5 4 3 2 1

Library of Congress Number: 2020943220
ISBN: 9780820358444 (paperback)
ISBN: 9780820358451 (ebook)

In memory of Michael David Goldman (1936–2010)
and David William Goldman (1962–93)

For my mother, Barbara Goldman

CONTENTS

ACKNOWLEDGMENTS

This book has been made possible by my father Michael Goldman's unbounded joy for his work as a scientist and his perhaps too unreserved confidence in my own capabilities as a researcher and writer. If he taught me to drive a car with a clutch in a parking lot with a degree of caution while advancing my twin brothers to roadways more quickly when it was their turn to be schooled, he never hesitated in pronouncing me ready to take on whatever intellectual challenge came my way. This confidence—misplaced or not—seems as great a gift to me in retrospect as it did when I was a sarcastic teenager. Just as importantly, my mother, Barbara Goldman, early shaped and encouraged my habits of reading across disciplines by offering me books from astronomy to art history that threw the world open while simultaneously always managing to speak urgently and directly to my interests. Her exquisite taste in books has remained a central influence. These days my writing occupies the end tables in her Portland living room. Her excitement when I tell her of a new publication is in itself sufficient reward for the work. My brother Charles, upon whom I foisted the more autobiographical portions of these essays in draft, forbore with great patience to correct what must seem to him to be my faulty memories of events. My sister, Susie, by offering her own point of view on the same sections, helped foster the kind of perspectival triangulation upon which storytelling (and science) thrive. My late brother, David—a soft-spoken but garrulous storyteller—did not live to see this book begun but even as a young man always supported my endeavors.

Many thanks to the National Endowment for the Humanities for providing a grant that helped sustain this project in its early stages and a We the People award that helped honor it.

My thanks also go to the *Georgia Review*, where earlier versions of "Stargazing in the Atomic Age," "Listening to Gershwin," and "Questions of Transport" first appeared; to the *Michigan Quarterly Review*, which published an earlier version of "In Praise of Bellow"; and to the *Southwest Review*, in whose pages an earlier version of "Leaving Russia: The Soulful Modernism of Chagall and Rothko" was published as "Soulful Modernism."

Longtime friends and colleagues Gillian Conoley, Kim Hester-Williams, Sherril Jaffe, Noelle Oxenhandler, and Greta Vollmer read portions of this book at its most nascent. Their early support of the project, and constant support of me, has been immensely sustaining. Brantley Bryant generously commented on "Questions of Transport," and Mike Ezra offered the same attention to "Wonderful World." Rabbi Alan Lew—if only he were still walking among us—reviewed the discussion of Talmudic study in "Stargazing in the Atomic Age" with his inimitable generosity. Miquel Salmeron, friend and physicist at the Lawrence Berkeley National Laboratory, vetted this essay and kindly prevented me from making any serious misrepresentations of his field. Aliette Mandelbrot, Benoit Mandelbrot's widow, provided similar service with respect to "Wonderful World: The Fractal Geometry of Benoit Mandelbrot." My thanks also go to Lynne Morrow, music director of Pacific Voices and the Oakland Symphony Chorus as well as my colleague at Sonoma State, who championed "Listening to Gershwin" from the outset and who introduced me to the extraordinary repertoire of the Oakland Symphony.

Having taught three (and, for a time, four courses a semester) at the same institution for over two decades, I have been fortunate to encounter a great many gifted student writers and critics. Would that I had noted from the outset of my teaching life at SSU these extraordinary people. Because I can no longer name them all, I will simply offer my appreciation to them as a group, registering fully what an honor it was to work with each and every individual.

Jesse Kercheval, as gifted a teacher as she is a writer, read "Listening to Gershwin" in draft and offered valuable advice. I am grateful as well to Patrick Madden for taking the time between writing and teaching to champion "Stargazing in the Atomic Age" and to offer encouragement during this book's earlier stages. I have taken heart more than once from Jonis Agee's wise suggestions as well as her encouragement and support of my writing generally. I deeply appreciate the intellectual camaraderie provided by Penny Wright and Ellen Siegelman—and of course by Mitzi McCloskey, who brought us together. Mitzi, I can still hear your gravelly, delighted laugh.

In addition to the longtime friends with whom I have worked at Sonoma State, I have been fortunate to have the support of family and friends whose collective care provided me with metaphorical (and sometimes literal) shelter. Thank you, Sandy Bulmash, Yanie Chaumette, Charles and Julie Goldman, Elke Jones, Margie and Butch and Jenny LeRoy, Manjari and Mike Lewis, Pam Mohr, Kim Overton and Carl Johnson, Chessie Rochberg, Bill and Betty Parsons, Connie Philipp, Renee Talmon, and new writing colleague Kathleen Winter. I continue to be inspired by Katy DiNatale, Maryam Majeed, Amrita Sengupta, and Nancy Sloan: brillant, kind, and courageous young women all.

I am grateful to Willard Spiegelman and Terri Lewers at the *Southwest Review* and Laurence Goldstein and Vicki Lawrence at the *Michigan Quarterly Review* for their editorial work on earlier versions of "Leaving Russia " and "In Praise of Bellow."

A multitude of thanks to the University of Georgia Press for all of their work seeing this book into print, and, in particular, to Walter Biggins and Beth Snead for taking on the project and to Jon Davies and Steven Wallace for seeing it through with aplomb during the pandemic. My gratitude goes as well to Susan Harris for excellent copyediting and to the very talented designer Erin Kirk for her beautiful cover design.

I owe an enormous debt to the entire staff at the *Georgia Review*—surely the most conscientious, perspicacious, and considerate of quarterly rosters—and in particular to Doug Carson and former managing editor Mindy Wilson for their work on "Stargazing in the Atomic Age" and "Listening to Gershwin." It has been an equal pleasure, more recently, to work with C. J. Bartunek. Likewise, it has been a very great blessing to work with now former editor Stephen Corey, whose questions and commentary always called attention to precisely those sentences whose imperfections, once improved, turned out to be key to the development of the essays of which they are a part. Thank you, Stephen, for championing my work from its earliest period and for the many hours you have put into these pages.

And finally, there is Zoë: brilliant scholar, gorgeous writer, sweetest of daughters. Thank you for being not only the best of company but for showing me that the "ideal reader"—in at least one case—need not remain a Platonic concept.

STARGAZING IN THE ATOMIC AGE

INTRODUCTION

When I started writing this book about Jewish American achievement in the twentieth century, I set out to counter the assumption that Jewish history chronicles only tragedy. I wanted to explore systematically what I knew in my heart to be true: that life in the United States for Jews has been characterized less by anguish than by tremendous drive and innovation. *Stargazing in the Atomic Age* takes the nadir of modern Jewish experience—the Holocaust—as its starting point, but it is far from elegiac. Part reflection and part critique, part intellectual history and part personal narrative, it celebrates artists and scientists who confronted the war years with exceptional energy. From the outset, as I cast around for illustration of accomplishment, I found it difficult not to locate examples but to limit their number. Everywhere I turned I was met by writers like Saul Bellow, who in *Humboldt's Gift* chastises Americans "spared the holocausts and nights of terror" and urges "with our advantages we should be formulating the new basic questions for mankind"; by musicians like Aaron Copland, who insisted in his 1952 Norton lectures at Harvard, "I must believe in the ultimate good of the world and of life as I live it in order to create a work of art"; and by scientists like Richard Feynman, who worked in Los Alamos on the Manhattan Project during the war, only to counsel a 1963 audience at the University of Washington: "It is better to say something and not be sure than not to say anything at all."

Throughout my grade school years, my father chided my liberal use of sarcastic speech with a different remonstration ("If you don't have anything nice to say, don't say anything at all"). Nonetheless, the household in which I grew up vibrated with the kind of speechified "somethings" Feynman fizzed with and that are the stock-in-trade of Bellow's high-spirited characters. My father, a medical researcher whose grandparents immigrated from Russia in the 1890s (the same decade George Gershwin's parents stepped upon U.S. shores), relished upending the ideas his peers assumed were inviolable in respiratory physiology. His eldest child, I was raised to take nothing for granted. Still, I was well into a draft of this book when I realized its characters shared my father's penchant for provocation. Seeking the most dazzling examples of contributions to science and the arts, I had unerringly chosen the work of men whose sensibilities conformed to the infuriating, enlivening, and inspiring milieu within which I had grown up.

And men these physicists, artists, composers, mathematicians, and writers turned out to be. In writing about Jewish innovation in America, I had created a collective biography of a paternal generation I knew firsthand. Few of its characters shared my father's predilection for fly-by-night schemes. But their vitality was the same élan that animated my family life, their lively (if sometimes self-absorbed) expressions of feeling the tones that had furthered the talk at our dinner table. Preferring challenging questions over practiced answers, they pushed against what was axiomatic in their fields as eagerly as they traveled in thought beyond the borders of these disciplines.

Most of the characters who walk through these pages are household names. My intent, however, has been to approach them from new angles. By defamiliarizing these icons through juxtaposition and unsettling our collective assumptions about them—what they did and what we think their contributions might "stand for"—I hope to reveal their personalities as more complex and their approaches as more intriguing. Consider Rothko's late canvases in light of the spare prose of Genesis. Hear echoes of the metaphysics of Maimonides in Einsteinian physics. Discover Montaigne's sixteenth-century concerns on death and dying voiced in altered key in the reveries of Bellow's characters, whose exuberant myopia does not prevent them from being ravished by the world's quotidian beauties.

Why assume that a familiarity with disaster invites despair to settle in for centuries? When Jerusalem's First Temple was left a pile of charred stones and its congregation found themselves among the hanging gardens of Babylon, the newly exiled did more than weep: they prospered, developing the Talmud over the course of the first millennium. Alexandria, Spain, Berlin, and New York: after every scattering, another golden age. The twentieth-century intellectuals featured in this book offer evidence of this pattern. Despite the political chaos through which they traveled, they hazarded connections, reaching toward the unknown as surely as Michelangelo's Adam extends his fingers across the vaulted Sistine Chapel. Frequently, absorbed in their work, they transformed "awful" into "awe."

Of course they understood the yearning for lost places. Some could not help but register nostalgia in the rueful cadences of their own accented speech. But like Grace Paley, Bronx-born daughter of Russian immigrants who reminds readers in "The Immigrant Story" that "rosiness is not a worse windowpane than gloomy grey when viewing the world," the generation who came of age during World War II understood that asking questions offers a fail-safe way to shake off melancholy. Deeply curious about the world despite its human tragedies, they did not so much resist the pull of the past as wrestle themselves away from it by setting themselves problems to solve.

Intellectual ferment sustains those who produce it. But the energy any creative act releases affirms life for the rest of us. Global political unrest, unparalleled natural disasters hurried along by Earth's rising temperatures, systemic extinction of chains of species—yes, these are our conditions of being. How else can we face the terror of our situation but by remaining open—now and in the future—to its possibilities? It would be foolish to echo Dustin Hoffman's character in Barry Levinson's prescient *Wag the Dog* and crow, "This is nothing!" But reminding ourselves how excitement over ideas sustained the artists and scientists of the previous century even as they stared straight ahead at the apocalypse might rally us. In the midst of a newly divisive era, the confidence with which these thinkers elaborated modes of understanding that defied partisanship and parochialism seems a remarkable kind of faith. Their staunchness, their refusal to give in to despair, their pleasure and astonishment in achievement—this strength of mind can be ours as well.

ICONOCLASM CON BRIO

A Reminiscence

From Minneapolis to Montana to Massachusetts, the houses my family inhabited in the 1960s were loud with the chatter and squall of four small children. If you chanced to visit, you might have watched my twin brothers glue parts onto each other's model airplanes or tear them apart in fury while our younger sister twirled to music and I sat with my legs curled on the island of our green armchair reading a book. Every so often my mother's breathless voice darted hummingbird-fashion through the clamor. Once my father returned from the hospital, it would have taken you only a moment to recognize this author of grand entrances and ostentatious exits as the conductor of our family's tone and tempo.

A decade later, with three children in high school and my mother beginning a master's degree in communications (who could blame her?), the talk at our table had swelled into a three-ring circus of competing conversations and knock-down, drag-out arguments. My siblings and I scrabbled vociferously for the spotlight. But my father's voice claimed center stage, rising to a teakettle pitch of incredulity as he exclaimed over some exceptional bureaucratic stupidity only to fall to the exaggeratedly low tones he used to chastise me—thrice over and at achingly slow speed—for deflecting his sermons with my flippant sardonic quips. (And still, the more deliberately he berated, the less I listened.)

Excitable and effusive, Dad could have stepped straight out of a Bellow novel. He was as lavish in grief as Tommy Wilhelm, as frantically openhearted as Herzog, as joyous as Ravelstein. Years after I left the family house and raised my own daughter, I needed only to pick up *Henderson the Rain King* to be returned to the cockamamie schemes of my childhood. After turning a few pages I was airlifted out of Africa to the Montana plains—a landscape that must have seemed no less strange to my midwestern-born parents. In this arid place back in 1964, my father had interrupted his fledgling scientific career in Minneapolis to serve a two-year stint as medical officer and captain in the air force. Once on base, he spent equal time attending patients and antagonizing his superiors. It took him little time to make a habit of defying their unofficial first commandment—"Rank has its privileges"—by sporting mismatched socks each morning and eating dinner with enlisted men rather than with his fellow officers. But he was not dressed down by the commander until he made a field trip to Congress while at a D.C. medical conference. Sen. Hubert Humphrey was "out" when Dad stepped into his office ready to complain about Glasgow's poor morale, but my father enlisted the sympathy of the politician's secretary, prescribing extensive dieting advice for her in the stentorian, teacherly voice he used to edify those in clinic anxious about their own conditions. When my family returned to Montana, Glasgow's upstart physician was met with a reception colder than a winter at Glacier National Park. While we goggled at early airplanes suspended like mobiles in the cavernous interior of the National Air and Space Museum, a four-star general had been marching through Glasgow to conduct a congressional investigation of the base.

Each time I return to Humboldt's rages and Herzog's emotionalism, I relive my father's arbitrary tempests and his embarrassingly teary moments. But I recognize his inexhaustible hopefulness in the panache with which Bellow's people shrug off defeat, pick up the pieces, and claim victory. When I began André Aciman's elegant memoir of an Alexandrian childhood cut short following the nationalization of the Suez Canal, I was startled to discover in the swaggering Turkish-born relative who monopolizes *Out of Egypt*'s opening chapter another figure much like Dad. Vili may strike many readers as flamboyant, but his dramatic posturing is eminently familiar to me. In the Mediterranean basin during World War II, Aciman's uncle had located Roman antiques and sold them at ten times their cost. At the end of the war, he changed his name, converted to Christianity, foreswore all other nationalities, and settled in Surrey. In the pages of Aciman's memoir, this character strides past the green lawns and well-kept gardens of the English countryside with no less complacency and vigor than any British-born figure clad in Harris Tweed.

My father took to camouflage with equal enthusiasm. While an undergraduate at Harvard, he changed his name to the generic American Mike, dispensing with Menachim Myron, an identity almost unpronounceable in Wisconsin. By the end of his freshman year, he had rejected the country ways he learned on his parents' cherry and apple orchard for East Coast irony. As diligently as those nineteenth-century greenhorns before him who memorized the Pledge of Allegiance before they disembarked from Ellis Island, my American-born father forgot his Russian Jewish birthright. I grew up in a household rich in talk and tirade but cannot remember him once volunteering an anecdote about his past. He kept no pictures of himself as a college student, much less as a small boy. He never talked about the reading and writing he must have undertaken in preparation for his bar mitzvah, even when his granddaughter was composing her own *drash*. A year before Zoë's bat mitzvah, he listened absently while she sang a prayer in her clear, pure voice as if he were hearing the chatter of an unknown tongue.

Dad was so eager to assimilate that he simply insisted on his own centrality. As soon as he arrived at Harvard, he settled into venerable Eliot House as if he owned its brick and wainscoting. Stumbling across an attractive armchair in the conference room, he requisitioned it for his dorm room without a second thought. The next day, students received a stiff note from the house master demanding the return of a five-hundred-dollar piece of furniture embossed with the college seal. At a black-tie dinner this resident fellow had hosted the evening before, a plastic chair had glared out like a neon sign for Pabst Blue Ribbon amid the elegant mahogany circling the table.

"Toujours, l'audace," Aciman writes of Vili. My father was equally undaunted, but he grew up among strangers rather than amid excitable relatives in cosmopolitan Alexandria. The lone Jewish boy in Sturgeon Bay, Dad attended school alongside children who spoke with stolid restraint in the careful, tuneful accents of their Scandinavian forebears. While my father and his sisters made their way through the quiet streets of this slow-moving town, André Aciman strolled along the Corniche, Alexandria's coastal highway, sipping a cooling drink made from rose water and nibbling on the fried sweet dough that marks the end of Ramadan—this in defiance of the Passover injunction against leavening.

Still, Vili and Michael are cousins cut from the same cloth, unabashed parvenus whose adoption of foreign custom never threatens their Jewish spirit. Both highlight a survival instinct in a culture that favors chameleons more than martyrs—changelings, that is, who pass to extricate themselves from a difficult spot or to obtain a better situation. Taking the train from Green Bay to begin college, my father must have known he was moving from a Midwest as far removed from Boston as the Middle East is from London. Still, he trespassed the Puritan halls of the university with arrogant aplomb. Later, during his years on the faculty at the Harvard School of Public Health, he thumbed his nose at the class pretensions of the Cambridge elite with no less glee, joking with colleagues who worked elsewhere that Harvard lopped 20 percent off the salaries it doled out "for prestige." With my mother and the four of us children in tow, he continued traversing the country. During a sabbatical year we spent in an apartment alongside London's Hampstead Heath, he delighted in mimicking the inflections of the British, imitating their disingenuous apologies and cheerily expectant commands—if with more fanfare than accuracy.

It would be child's play for me to fashion Dad as the last in a string of beleaguered Jewish wanderers destined for a lifetime of looking through windows. But this sad state of affairs was far from the truth. He might have been unsuccessful at permanent stays, but my father was never the melancholic exile of conventional histories. Irremediably energetic and chronically hostile to despair, he continued to cut a picaresque figure wherever he traveled. He took up research positions in Cleveland and Phoenix, breezed through Salt Lake City and Los Angeles, and careened from Paris to Amarillo, puzzling over the way human lungs work all the while. In 2010, on a birthday visit to my daughter, he quieted Zoë's fears about her asthma by explaining the mechanics of breathing to her with the same patient intelligence he had once dispensed diet tips to Senator Humphrey's secretary. Then, never one to waste a good research subject, he handed his granddaughter the mouthpiece of his equipment so that he could obtain more data for an ongoing study.

Many scientists scale back their efforts in the lab as they age, assuming their most brilliant work lies behind them. Not Dad: he wrote as many grants in his late sixties and early seventies as he finished the decade before. During the spring of 2010, when he was seventy-three, he arrived at what he felt was his most groundbreaking discovery. As he typed away on his computer in my dining room during what would be his last visit, he called me to his side. Pointing to a tangle of colored lines he had graphed on the shimmering screen, he announced, in a voice slightly mellower but no less excited than the forty-years-younger timbre I had listened to as a child, that he had solved a problem that would make his name. Three weeks later, after hiking up the hill in back of his Los Angeles home with a colleague and during whose duration Dad had predictably spent discussing his forthcoming paper, his heart stopped and the inhalations and exhalations of his own lungs ceased.

Some would call this spectacular bad timing. I wave away pathos, preferring to retell stories of his peregrinations and pitfalls in the conquering major key of C. The father who screamed himself hoarse in the family car in five minutes flat and who sardined his four children in a camper designed for two on a three-week tour of Scotland was the same man who navigated the taxi-clotted metropolis of London without a single wrong turn, despite a night's missed sleep and a steering wheel placed on what even my nine-year-old sister knew was the wrong side of the car. A fish out of water, he was perpetually convinced the absence of other swimmers advertised their lack of staying power rather than his own confusion. He took up each new research appointment with the fervor of a man beginning his honeymoon and, chronically hostile to despair, faced every obstacle with unshakeable confidence in its eventual obliteration.

A similar dauntlessness prompted Chagall to travel to Paris to learn an art forbidden by family and faith and provoked Einstein to stretch space in pursuit of new physical laws. A like ironic temperament goaded Feynman to perfect his safecracking techniques in the heart of the high-security complex of wartime Los Alamos. I admire such defiance of difficulty. Older now, I understand that a willful refusal to give up is as much triumph as most of us are likely to achieve. There is something glamorously insolent in choosing to face each wave with the same eagerness as the current dragging you toward your starting place. We think people hopeless when we call them incorrigible, but aren't there at least some instances when we should applaud their irrepressible curiosity? My father never looked back. Instead, translating unspoken grief into forward motion as did the artists and scientists in these pages, he hurried onward—panting, sometimes wheezing, but always calling with insistent, unmitigated perseverance for confirmation.

DISLOCATION AND INVENTION

A Fugue

In between theorizing general relativity and developing the cosmological constant, Albert Einstein played chamber music. An accomplished amateur, his appreciation took shape not just in attentive listening but also in a warm tone and well-chosen fingerings. He stopped taking formal lessons as a teenager, but the violin he considered his greatest source of joy accompanied him to Zurich, where he was schooled; to the patent office at Bern, where he developed the special theory of relativity; to the University of Prague, where he took up a professorship; and then across the wide Atlantic to Princeton, where in 1940, having been stateless since World War I, he was naturalized but never trusted. (His FBI file runs over a thousand pages.) For the rest of his life, beginning in 1933, Einstein spent his days at the university's Institute for Advanced Study investigating problems in quantum mechanics. Evenings he devoted to Mozart, at the white frame house on Mercer Street close to campus. In a 1944 interview with the *New York Times*, Einstein avowed his reverence for the composer by calling Mozart's sound "so pure" it provides "a reflection of the inner beauty of the universe."

Einstein is not the only Jewish intellectual featured in this book to insist upon Mozart's singularity. Saul Bellow (another Nobel Prize winner) paid the prodigy homage twice over—first, when he delivered "Mozart: An Overture" as the keynote speech at the composer's bicentennial, and again, when he selected this essay as overture to *It All Adds Up*, his own 1994 nonfiction collection. Mark Rothko understood Mozart less as accompaniment to painting than "the alpha and omega" of his art, son Christopher indicates in *Mark Rothko: From the Inside Out*. The artist would not so much as pick up a brush before first unsleeving a Mozart LP and setting it on the turntable in his studio.

Mathematician and self-titled "fractalist" Benoit Mandelbrot names Mozart along with Verdi the composers he most esteems in an *Edge* interview with Hans Ulrich Obrist—"but not Wagner that much." And musicologist Alfred Einstein echoes the physicist, who was perhaps his distant cousin, when he pronounces Mozart so preternaturally gifted as to be not "of this world." Mozart was not—could not be—"truly at home" anywhere, Alfred Einstein goes on to suggest in *Mozart: His Character, His Work*, a 1945 text that remains on the shortlist of major contributions to Mozart studies. Having fled Munich before the start of the Second World War, it is not surprising that he implicitly aligned his own resettlements with the Salzburg composer's perpetual travel across states while arguing that Mozart's rootlessness was inextricable from his greatness.

Like both Einsteins, Mozart was disinherited by the city he left as a young man. Though he was renowned throughout Europe, Salzburg guidebooks published five and six years after his 1791 death contain no mention of this native son: no reference to his early years, biographer Maynard Solomon tells us, no plaque identifying the home or the street of his birth, no encomiums to the performances in cathedrals and salons where Mozart conducted the compositions that still play in our ears, their notes undegradable and brilliant as stars. To be fair, after traipsing from Munich to Mannheim and Paris to Prague as a child in the company of sister Nannerl (violinist) and father, Leopold (first music director), Mozart retained little love and less respect for his birthplace. Its natives were "intolerable" and its court musicians "coarse," "slovenly," and "dissolute."[1] "One hears nothing" in Salzburg, Mozart wrote unfeelingly to a friend who remained there (but with what Saul Bellow identifies in his Mozart essay as a "novelist's gift of characterizing by minute particulars"). For this composer, Salzburg was a musical limbo devoid not just of theater but also of opera—because singers, after all, would "insist on being handsomely paid, and generosity is not one of our faults." While Mozart chafed at the town's pettiness, he was no more impressed with Vienna, the city that would become the base for his adult expeditions after he rebelled against his employer, the Archbishop of Salzburg, and was immediately dismissed. There in Vienna in 1791—thirteen years after the composer's epistolary swipes at the lesser

1   All citations from the 1985 *The Letters of Mozart and His Family*, translated and edited by Emily Anderson, are drawn from Maynard Solomon's *Mozart: A Life* (New York: HarperCollins, 1995), except where noted otherwise.

lights of Salzburg's concert stages—he dictated eight bars of his *Requiem*'s "Lacrimosa" and drew his last breath.

What makes Mozart peerless? The elixir of grace notes and rising cadences he offers without letting us forget the pulses that pull us down to Earth? The cosmopolitan charm with which he travels back and forth between languages in his vocal music? The curious lightness in the darker tones of the andantes and adagios that speak suffering without ponderousness? Maybe it is the fine eighteenth-century control, one so effortlessly achieved it seems all measure and no weight, with which Mozart balanced melancholy and exuberance. Or maybe it is just the pragmatic in him that appealed to artists and scientists who fled Germany and France—places he played—during a period of tremendous conflict and uncertainty. Like Jane Austen, an artist of his own generation, Mozart offers effervescence without effusion. Tincturing ecstasy with irony, he glances at delight without ever wallowing in sentiment. (Can we even feel enchantment without simultaneously registering its transience?)

Certainly Mozart exploits an irony as keen as Austen's in *Così Fan Tutte* (my own favorite opera). Not even Shakespeare leaps as nimbly over the chasm between ideal and actual as does Mozart, who soothes our roiling feelings by cataloguing all of love's discord—hypocrisy, betrayal, flattery, vanity, and inconstancy—in a musical language so exquisite no verbal tribute could equal its harmonies. Bellow, who wisely leaves off commending this work almost before he begins, is satisfied to call *Così Fan Tutte* a "miracle." The composer "was not obliged to seek the truth in German, French, Italian, or English. His objective was not sincerity; it was bliss." As if echoing Alfred Einstein, Bellow, the Quebec-born child of Russian immigrants, praises Mozart's immunity to the parochial. Here, as in Einstein's 1945 study, Mozart appears to be an Austrian who isn't one—or rather, the kind of Austrian both the fiction writer and the musicologist wished all that country's citizens might be.

In attributing such thinking to Bellow and Alfred Einstein, I veer perilously close to ethnocentrism. Nonetheless, it is worth remembering that in the middle of the twentieth century the Austrian most on the world's mind was not this or any other composer but the art student who had dropped canvas and easel in favor of demolition. An expatriate thanks to the Third Reich, Alfred Einstein contemplated Europe's broken girders and twisted steel from afar. Nationalism was devouring millions in Europe as his Mozart book went to press. "A Wartime Book" designated by Oxford University Press in New York as one "produced in full compliance with the government's regulations for conserving paper and other essential materials," the study focuses less upon the practical difficulties Mozart's itinerary must have created than upon the composer's gloriously rebellious independence from regional and imperial authorities. How could this Salzburg-born but widely ranging prodigy—a free spirit if ever there was one—not offer Alfred Einstein and his readers lessons in survival amid the smoking ruins of the twentieth century's hearths?

Rereading this book three-quarters of a century after its publication summons Mozart for me as a slight, pale, pockmarked man scrawling crescendos and diminuendos on rag paper. Beside him, hovering shadowy as the diminutive suns children capture on the ground during eclipses with makeshift cameras, Albert Einstein speaks in his thickly accented English, chalking equations on a blackboard in tidy script. Even as his mathematical expressions revealed the design of the cosmos, the officials in charge of his homeland's security shrank the territory within which "non-Aryans" were permitted to move. In 1933, not long after Germany outlawed all political blocs but the Nazi Party, Albert Einstein left its ever-narrowing space. I see his wife, Elsa, looking out over the water after boarding the Red Star Line's *Westernland* in Southampton alongside her celebrated husband, her free hand clinging to the rails, her round face flushed, her fine hair frizzing below the edges of a black hat perched jauntily to one side. What must these two of have said to each other as the boat left its moorings?

Dislocation is debilitating, but it can also spur innovation. Einstein knew this. So did Mozart, an itinerant who made a virtue out of necessity. "Without travel, one is a miserable creature," the composer wrote to the father who wished to chain him to Salzburg's provincial rhythms. In another letter to Leopold, Mozart, who never ceased attempts to be a good son, returned to this conflict. A mediocre person stays undistinguished whether he travels or stays at home, the composer insisted by way of rationale for his resettlements. But the person of superior talents ("which I cannot deny myself to have without being blasphemous," he cannot help adding with inimitable élan), will become "bad, if he always stays in the same place."[2] Not long after, Mozart decamped to Paris, despite his father's guilt-inducing objections, taking his ailing mother with him to oblige his other parent. When she died there under winter's cold

2   This correspondence is cited by Peter Gay in *Mozart: A Life* (New York: Viking, 1999).

skies, Mozart continued working, answering loss with music, translating indefinable wistfulness into a yearning at once cerebral and soulful.

The bright tone of the violin was for a time displaced by the viola's deeper timbre. A "kind of longing, which is never satisfied"—such was loneliness, he would write ten years later, this time during a separation from his wife.

Einstein's own perspicacious ear heard longing as well as delight in the cadences of Mozart, fellow traveler. During the war that forced him to turn his back upon his childhood memories, the scientist—world traveler and time voyager, seer into the twisted warp and woof of the universe—sat in a small house at the edge of a field in New Jersey playing Mozart's violin sonata in E minor. Where else for a Jew born into twentieth-century Europe to draw solace? Not in a distinct geography or a particular historical era but amid key signatures and time signatures of a different order. "I live my daydreams in music. I see my life in terms of music," Einstein offered in a 1929 *Saturday Evening Post* interview. Studying the vastness of space must have palliated the residual nostalgia he felt on this pearl of a planet for the sounds of his youth: the southern inflections of Bavarian speech, the clock on the steeple that chimed the quarter hour in Bern under which he used to grant patents, the yawl of the approaching train horn that bent in pitch as the engine retreated outside his office. But more than such memories, music provided Einstein the right of return. Mozart came home to Salzburg when he crafted *The Magic Flute*, an opera as modern in its burlesque of German custom and manners as the impudent satire of Weimar Republic cabaret. Two hundred years later, the crystalline inflections of *Die Zauberflöte* restored to Einstein the language the Second World War left his family no reason to use.

The work of the physicist is to measure the incalculable. There is the beauty of solutions and the beauty that cannot be fathomed. Einstein spent the large measure of his waking hours thinking through forces that remain mostly unreckoned. Ultimately, it was mystery rather than certainty that arrested him—in music as in math. An art of concordance, music bespeaks the exquisitely tuned relationships that hold the planets in their orbits, the stars in the sky, and us, marvels of molecular engineering, in our own skins. A psalm that reconnects the wandering self to the world in the largest sense, music gestures outward through intangibles of feeling, encouraging our attention to stray beyond the walled lines that divide nation-states toward the shimmering curve of Earth's atmosphere.

Is there a way in which the laws of music parallel the mathematical principles contemporary cosmologists use to figure the shape of the universe Einstein began to make out? Maybe such a correspondence is only my romantic fancy. Still, I would bargain that more than one scientific thinker is prompted now and again by Mozart, that other wandering star. Even those of us who appear blank in the face of physics know that the circumlocutions of water molecules follow the pull of the moon two hundred thousand miles distant from Earth's oceans. Is it so strange to imagine that the musical phrases amplified in our cars and rooms and earphones might call us all toward the velvet darkness of much farther shores?

ANTECEDENT

The Energy of Exodus

Few readers of Lamentations forget its dark incandescent beauty. Story of the Babylonian captivity—the first Jewish Diaspora—the poem cries out grief from opening elegy to final entreaty. "What can I match with you to console you, / O Fair Maiden Zion?" its writer wonders before proposing a figure of uncontainable catastrophe for answer: "For your ruin is vast as the sea."[1] The line is clear and supple as water, lucent even in despair. The waste conjured here absorbs space and time. Eternal rather than temporal, it is boundless as the waves that issue beyond the horizon to batter the shore at our feet.

How startling, then, to find the Bible's foundational narrative of exile and enslavement replete with everything *but* mourning. Arguably the most important portion of the Torah, Exodus offers a paradigm for Jewish cycles of expulsion and return. Religious and secular Jews alike recite it every year at Passover. One of the most ancient liturgical texts in the Bible, its "Song of the Sea" remains part of the routine of daily prayer. But the language of this book shares little, tonally speaking, with Lamentations. No "Alas" sighs out from its pages. No wails sob into silence. No breathy flute or pallid lute strums quietly to the cadence of bereavement. Line after line resonates with energy, verve, and direction. One chapter in the book's forty recounts the backbreaking work the Jews perform as slaves. The rest provide blueprints not for razing, but for building: instructions for constructing the Tabernacle—the Israelites' traveling desert sanctuary—as well as the costumes of those who will worship within it.

---

1   All citations from Lamentations are drawn from the *Jewish Study Bible*, edited by Adele Berlin, Mark Zvi Brettler, and Michael Fishbane (New York: Oxford University Press, 2004).

If nothing else, the elaborate descriptions of construction materials that occupy the middle verses of this book (a liturgical owner's manual many readers are understandably quick to gloss over) foreground both the energy of creation and its beauty. Genesis chronicles how God separates wind from water and populates Earth with its startling diversity of fauna, fruits, and flowers. Exodus recalls these generative acts using a human scale. Gilded wood, a hammered lamp, flower-shaped cups: scores of verses command the itinerant congregation to create. Make the Tabernacle cloth of "fine twisted linen, blue, purple, and crimson yarns," they are directed; make its table of "acacia wood" overlain "with pure gold, inside and out"; make its lampstand "of hammered work" with "three cups shaped like almond-blossoms, each with calyx and petals, on one branch." As for the priestly vestments: each should fashion a breast piece set with amethyst and emerald, chrysolite and crystal, agate, jasper, lapis lazuli—stones of Earth brilliant as the tribes they betoken.

This second book of the Torah is full of noisy activity and determined movement. Decisive and absolute, God's voice rends the air as an earthquake shears through ground. Sound waves roil the sky and pound the earth, setting Mount Sinai to a violent trembling. The horn trumpets the Lord's thunder, its pitch increasing to an earsplitting volume as God approaches. And the people subjected to this boom and blast? Forget keening (if not kvetching): during their Egyptian enslavement, their years in the wilderness, and their days encamped at the foot of Sinai, the travelers have too much work to do to spare time for sobbing. Many twentieth- and twenty-first-century memoirs of exile follow the pattern Lamentations establishes, adopting an attitude of stillness rather than struggle. But such sadness demands leisure to express. The displaced persons of Exodus do not reflect. They only follow along behind God as if they were small children skip-stumbling to keep pace with their father's longer stride.

Each time I read this book, I trail along as they work and whine, listen and learn, rebel and resolve anew. Exodus is awash in blood and anger, but it is driven as well by a strong sense of urgency and purpose. I feel fear but also witness faith; I recognize dread but also register awe. Granted, the sixth chapter describes "spirits . . . crushed by cruel bondage." But I cannot picture the Jews as a broken people here. Did they drop to their knees with the weight of their burdens? Did they tear their hair in sorrow at the hopelessness of their condition? Perhaps, but Exodus does not say so. With the exception of that solitary line, I find little of resignation or despair in the book's language. Nor do I see the Israelites bending to the yoke. Disciplined and reproved, they remain, as their exasperated God attests, a "stiffnecked people."

They are also not souls who suffer in silence, as the voluble among their descendants would be quick to admit. Reading rhetorical questions like this one: "Why did you bring us up from Egypt, to kill us and our children and our livestock with thirst?" recalls the unanswerable "Nu?" of these peoples' Yiddish-speaking progeny. In their penchant for melodrama (they describe themselves less as famished than as constantly at the brink of extinction) I hear the expressive energy of their descendants. "If only we had died by the hand of the Lord in the land of Egypt, when we sat by the fleshpots, when we ate our fill of bread! For you have brought us out into this wilderness to starve this whole congregation to death," they groan to Moses.

How often, growing up, were those reproachful accents drummed emphatically upon my ear? "I have had a *bellyful* of your complaining," my father would begin, stretching the three-syllabled noun past its breaking point. "I've had it up to HERE!" his voice swelled as he continued, accompanying his diatribes by thumping a hand theatrically and percussively upon his heart. Moses's response ("What shall I do with this people? Before long they will be stoning me!") sounds so like the shrug-shouldered commentaries I hear in my head that I can only smile in recognition when I read these lines. Watch one of the early Woody Allen comedies or listen to a Seinfeld episode and you'll be treated to interrogatives that culminate in a similar flourish.

Moses may be the most revered man in the Torah, but his habit of complaint connects rather than distinguishes him from the unruly group who grudgingly attend his words. Grumbling is the hallmark of this mass who cannot resist puncturing each and every rhetorical balloon that threatens to inflate itself into pomposity. The "whole congregation" prostrates itself at God's approach, bowing low before Him. But in my mind's eye, even as their foreheads reach the dust, a man swivels his neck to the right, raises his eyebrows under his bent head, and rolls his eyes in exaggerated sufferance at a friend. Such imagined comedy—and I do believe Exodus offers not just plenty of puns but some actual funny moments—cannot but appeal to skeptics. The schtick we stumble across in this foundational text of the Bible as well as in stand-up points to an abiding knack for self-critique. Humor provides a saving sense of perspective, a making light and making small of those concerns that, looming large in our vision, threaten to hide the stones, tree roots, and broken side-walks before our feet.

The chosen people are alternately selected for God's special consideration and singled out for exceptional punishment. Such vertiginous swings between hubris and humility make for riveting drama. Equally impressive is this book's plot. No surprise that Exodus has provided a plumb line for classic and contemporary cinema, or that its story of action and adventure demands as much from its principal characters as any blockbuster exacts from overworked stuntmen. Yet the special effects Exodus creates surpass anything dreamed up by George Lucas or Steven Spielberg. Moses walks past a bush that bursts into flame and waves a rod that slithers out of his hand as a serpent. Next, he communicates the "extraordinary chastisements" the Egyptians will suffer should their sovereign not bow to the Lord's command—and not by way of a midlevel scribe ensconced in a dusty vestibule in the least-trafficked portion of the royal palace. Instead, Moses confronts the fleshly deity himself, Pharaoh glittering and fierce eyed in cloth-of-gold robe.

The splendor of this confrontation arrests me long after I close the book. I think back to Seders I have attended and see the drops of Manischewitz the tip of my index finger dribbled upon my plate, spotting its white ceramic, each small red circle standing in for a progressively more terrible plague. What imagination can resist the colored and impassioned vision of this story? In my mind's eye, blood clouds the water of the Nile as the women collect their washing, the dank river smell in their nostrils mixing with the rust of blood. Aaron holds out his arm, staff in hand, and earth's dust moves with the crawl-ing legs of lice. The insects creep through hair and burrow into clothing and raise welts on bare skin. Soon the bodies of cattle and horses and sheep bloat and rot in the sun. After the soot from the kiln Moses throws toward the sky washes down in a filthy rain, boils as big as fists break out on women and children and men, and Pharaoh's magicians are laid low. Next, the air thickens with storm, and hailstones streak to the ground, flattening trees and crushing the tender green of new growth. "Hold out your arm toward the sky," the Lord says to Moses, "that there may be darkness upon the land of Egypt, a darkness that can be touched." And darkness comes in a swarm of locusts that blacken the noon air until it vibrates with the whine of their wings.

The death of children, fast as the onset of fever; the massing of refugees who stream past columns painted with lotus flowers and trot past gilded sphinxes trundling carts heaped with chipped pots and stained linens; the great wall of water drawing itself high over the heads of soldiers too mesmerized to turn and run—the marvelous descriptions in the Torah's verse stir equal portions of fear and wonder. Here indeed is the language of shock and awe, a muscular idiom that shares nothing with the serene murmurings of more recent exilic stories whose nostalgia glows in sunset shades. Reading them, you might hear yearning twine around their quiet musings. But you will obtain none of the jagged angry energy that moves through the sentences of Exodus the way wind sweeps waves across water, the prose darkening as a sky thickens with thunderheads, the verses stabbing the air and coursing downward lightning-like in your imagination before they ground themselves in the paper your fingers turn.

Only at the end of this tumultuous book, when the air begins to clear, is it possible to feel something of the stillness kindred to Lamentations. "When Moses had finished the work, the cloud covered the Tent of Meeting, and the Presence of the LORD filled the Tabernacle. . . . When the cloud lifted . . . the Israelites would set out, on their various journeys." But the tranquility in this passage has nothing to do with dreary inactivity, that torpid immobility of conclusion. Nor should the Israelites' "various journeys" be confused with modern memories of disembarkations, descriptions of ships that keel across the water while their passengers turn wistfully toward the cityscapes from which these vessels are pulling away. Instead, on this day in Exodus, the people simply pick themselves up, gather their children once more, and walk out again.

STARGAZING IN THE ATOMIC AGE

1. "What do *you* care what other people think?"

When I was a girl, my father's behavior in the Boston suburb we lived in struck me as weird. His volatility was embarrassing. His emotionalism was out of place. He was a Rachmaninoff cadence where everyone else played Mozart, a medieval gargoyle perched atop a Lutheran church, a mai tai in the midst of the odorless, colorless gin and tonics that were Boston's favorite drink. When I grew up and moved away, I recognized his eccentricity for what it was—the incomplete conversion of this assimilated Jew, all quick, erratic motion and nervous energy, to the phlegmatic chill of New England. Where Dad worked, at the Harvard School of Public Health, the atmosphere was cool as the inside of a church—as were the faculty, several of whom he had roomed with at Eliot House ten years earlier but never dined alongside, since the university's eating clubs in the 1950s were strictly segregated. In their spacious Cambridge houses they remained secluded, the graceful curves of high brick walls separating their jade lawns from the jangly street traffic of nearby Harvard Square.

In the context of the city's strict composure, an uprightness that hoarded physical energy as if every movement were a waste of vital spirit, my dad's Jewish exuberance must have seemed shockingly flamboyant. And indeed, he was all violent activity: he screamed himself hoarse when we squabbled in the car, darted across streets before the "WALK" sign, rifled wildly through the stacks of papers in his office searching for the document he had stashed in some forgotten place because it was "important," huffed his way through car dealerships when some hapless salesman offered statistics that contradicted the basic laws of physics, ate too much from the party trays his Harvard colleagues nibbled from, and blew in to our house at the end of the day—disheveled but triumphant as some Greek general returning home at the end of the Trojan War.

Ignoring my mother's demurrals, my dad typically wore sneakers on the several occasions each year when our family drove into the city to hear the Boston Symphony Orchestra. He commented with gleeful sarcasm on whatever stupidity passed for convention and took the talk of car mechanics more seriously than the abstracts of some of his colleagues, who massaged their data, he felt, rendering their experiments unethical and valueless at a stroke. He spoofed Harvard's sanctimonious dinner parties in the mock prayer with which he inaugurated family suppers ("Good food, good meat, good God let's eat"). And, aggressively competitive, he never missed an opportunity to let the more socially conscious faculty of the School of Public Health know by example that their inherited facility among the intellectual elite could not stand up to his own uncouth, native brilliance.

Years later, reading Nobel Prize winner Richard Feynman's memoir, *"Surely You're Joking, Mr. Feynman!,"* I recognized in this physicist's indifference to social protocol and his failure to suffer fools gladly a "curious character" like my dad. Feynman, too, had a low tolerance for mediocrity. A physicist friend at the Lawrence Berkeley Labs remembers that the Nobel winner refused, point-blank, to attend meetings: they were fine for his colleagues, he thought, but his own brain was too valuable to idle away in committee. This pronouncement must have met with a mixed reception, but it was delivered with Feynman's usual aplomb. The anecdote he recounted as a new graduate student at Princeton might have been one of my father's own. Feynman could sniff out pretentiousness like a police dog trained to find street drugs; at Princeton, he found plenty of grandiloquence. The university was "an imitation of an English school" complete with phony British accents. The "Mahstah of Residences . . . was a professor of 'French littrachaw'" who invited him to a tea party—at which he distinguished himself in his inimitable Jewish way. Asked whether he would like cream or lemon in his tea, the scientist replied "'I'll have both, thank you,'" at which the stricken dean's wife could only manage, "Surely you're *joking*, Mr. Feynman." Here was Dad—except that he, as all four of us children knew, would have asked for five spoons of sugar too.

I have inherited my father's contempt for pieties. Ceremonies of all kinds make me squirm: I satirize homilies at weddings and funerals with whispered aspersions, as if to consent to ritual were to surrender independence of mind.

Of course this irreverence made for a stormy childhood, since the edicts I resisted most were my father's. But defiance of tradition is my birthright: hard to break. I am, after all, my father's daughter. I have absorbed his Jewish habits of mind. Because I spent my school years within the shadow of the Old North Church, however, I associate observance with New England culture rather than with Jewish orthodoxy. Two hundred years after the Revolutionary War, the tree-lined streets of Concord and Lexington wind in serpentine curves past stands of pine and the occasional field of corn left intact as a rural reminder of two centuries before. School trips prompted us to recall "our" heritage: the smallish boulder on the edge of the windswept coast that was Plymouth Rock, the cotton-smocked women who dipped candles and made soap from lye in perennial re-creation of Salem's Puritan past. Route 126, once a dirt path Paul Revere traveled on his Midnight Ride, is choked now with traffic from the burgeoning computer industry. The Daughters of the American Revolution still organize an annual restaging of the Revolutionary War hero's call to arms. Each year, the bugle call dragged me from sleep in the early morning hours. I woke to the harsh cry of the riders through the field behind our house and the hurried clacking of horseshoes on the tarred road outside: a small group of men in the costume of 1776 galloping by as if time had folded over itself in some quaint history book illustration of Einstein's theory.

Piety for me is Anglo-Protestant, Boston's choleric interpretation of its British inheritance: Cromwell's humorlessness, the starched white collars of eighteenth-century merchants whose portraits hang in the colonial wing of the Boston Fine Arts Museum—and the prim, moralizing gaze their grand-children's grandchildren turned upon my voluble family when our excited conversation troubled their polite restaurant murmurings. To be pious was to be dutiful, whether in dress or at prayer, at cocktail parties or school functions. Piety meant proper conduct, form rather than substance, the icy sangfroid of decorum. I favored irreverence because it allowed me a small rebellion against this incurious citizenry, as parsimonious of gesture as they were of speech. For a people who valued social compliance above all else, gaudiness was god-lessness, brashness an unpardonable sin. Talking with your hands was showy, vulgar, gauche. It was what my father called, in the loud drawl he designated as parody, "taaaacky," the very word itself too outré for Bostonians to utter.

When I watched my father speak to my classmates' parents on those few occasions when school functions brought us all together, I read in their slight stiffening the checked but palpable hostility this constricted social world exhibits toward the unreserved. My father's conversational brio distinguished him as unerringly as if he were wearing Joseph's coat. To New England eyes, he must have seemed honky-tonk as a neon sign blaring its advertisement for Budweiser, a loud macaw, a blotch of scarlet in the midst of their graceful monochrome of silvery birches, white-painted churches, and wrought-iron weather vanes tempered dusty black.

Growing up, I detested this obtrusiveness. Now, living some three thousand miles away from Boston's Back Bay, I realize that his expansive gesturing and mercurial speech, like his cocky disregard for convention, were inherited from his eastern European predecessors, themselves viewed askance by the Russians, Germans, and Poles they lived alongside. Strong emotion hovers like static electricity over his head. But so, too, does intellectual inquisitiveness, a respect for brilliance—whether in the field of automobile mechanics or theoretical physics—and a refusal to assume that established custom is inherently virtuous. My father's imperviousness to the glamour of the politic and his lack of obeisance to institutional authority constitute a principle pure as faith. Admiration for innovation, curiosity unfettered by the worship of long-established theory, and pleasure in scholarly epiphany that shatters intellectual tradition without a second's regret define his attitude toward work, as they typify the work of Jewish scientists more generally. Dad taught us that the only way to arrive at new ideas was to be a maverick. But his irreverence is less the product of "the scientific method" than of a Jewish tradition he shelved and largely "forgot," or rather, translated into an ostensibly nonpartisan affinity for Freud, Kafka, and Rilke—like many other secular Jews who find themselves living in uncongenial social climates. Framed within the wake of the World War II history that perpetually cautioned where it did not silence, this brashness is defiance; a refusal to prostrate the self before the unsympathetic gaze of the intolerant.

II. Apocalyptic Time

As a Rorschach test, the coupling of "Jews" with "modernity" is hardly ambiguous. Out of the inkblot, one picture habitually resolves: the Shoah, the second of the century's genocides. Two decades after World War II, the Holocaust became the pivot point upon which Jewish intellectual life turned. It remains, today, more than a half century later, the hinge upon which our sense of ourselves depends. Its wake of loss and erasure paradoxically solders American Jews together as a religious and cultural community. But the Holocaust has become the black hole of our history, swallowing the time-space within which it unfolds. Every narrative we produce today must bend and twist to accommodate this central force. If in ancient times we were treated to miracles and monarchs (King David, the burning bush, the plagues in Egypt, Joseph's prophetic dreams), the twentieth century brings only ash, quiet as snowfall.

In the past we had heroes, we had warriors, we had lovers—Solomon, the Song of Songs, the lilt of the lute, and the backward glance of the maiden. Rebecca, Deborah, Judah Maccabee. I was raised without these stories. Instead, like many of my secular contemporaries, I have come to know Jewishness as a badge of suffering, an ethnic "knowledge" ironically echoing Germany's yellow star. Like it or not, my iconography is the victim's, informed by photographs of people in the Warsaw Ghetto and in the death camps, through whose darkly intelligent eyes we see a prescient knowledge of their own erasure. In some sense the memorials we have constructed to the dead merely strengthen the pull this central sadness exerts upon us. Each visit to a museum, designed to honor our ancestors, reminds us as well of the inescapability of our fate as outsiders.

Such witnessing, in those of us temporally distant enough to be immune from fear, is an upwelling of Job's pride. Like William Faulkner's Anse Bundren, the patriarch of *As I Lay Dying*, we seem proud of being chosen for special misery. Pale eyes glued open in the "pleased astonishment" of the plagued unfortunate, Bundren repeats a mantra—"if ever was such a misfortunate man"—that could be our own. Faulkner's humor reveals the particular patterning of race conflict as it takes shape in the American South. The writer censures the way both Blacks and whites accept tragedy as their portion: dumbly unreflective as oxen, they keep their shoulders to the plow in assent to their twin Fates. Bundren is a comical figure whose complacency in the face of his family's endless calamities Faulkner vilifies, but his smugness finds an uncomfortable parallel in our readiness to anticipate perpetual trauma.

Habituated to understanding the modern period as allegorical of Jewish suffering, writing about achievement seems not so much difficult as blasphemous. Images of what Elaine Scarry calls "the body in pain" have crowded out alternate representations so fully that, come time to write this essay upon relationships between Jews as victims of war and Jews as engineers of war's most devastating technology to date, I initially found myself hard pressed to scratch out more than a few solitary paragraphs. "The cataclysm of murder and atrocity that we call the Holocaust is inescapable and indelible," Cynthia Ozick argues in "Tradition and the Jewish Writer," a 2005 essay. Sixty years after its end, the Shoah "inevitably marks—stains—our moral nature," she continues, as if conferring memorial tattoos upon her readers.

The unfortunate side effect of Paul Célan's brilliant, jet-like poetry is to absorb into its darkness the happier ghosts of the twentieth century. We remember the bitter irony of "Todesfuge": "He whistles his Jews into rows has them shovel a grave in the ground / he commands us play up for the dance." But all the others—the painters, the violinists, the chemists, the novelists, the surgeons, the architects, the engineers, the physicists—are forgotten, left without burial. To end this ceaseless listening to the dead feels hard, but I wish to honor our achievements, not the specious dignity we claim for the victim, and to offer my daughter another way to see, transporting her from the memory of Auschwitz toward Einstein and Feynman, as well as her grandfather—people whose unkillable drive to understand is shared by those lost to history.

iii. Relativities

Escape artists invented the atom bomb. Nazis destroyed European Jewry, and then the remnants of European Jewry became destroyers of worlds. Here is Albert Einstein, with his teasing smile and Charlie Chaplin eyes, caught by the camera: the Houdini of nuclear physics. Bright lights and fearsome acts, the magicians of World War II, the scientists of the Manhattan Project, strike a pose in Los Alamos. There is Hungarian-born Edward Teller, who fled Germany, at once irascible and charming. In the corner the retiring Emilio Segrè, his shadowed face inclined toward earth, a refugee from Italy. The young Otto Robert Frisch, who edged out of Denmark just as the Germans invaded. Wolfgang Pauli, who worked with Niels Bohr in his Copenhagen lab but left Europe between the wars. Alongside them are ranged the Americans J. Robert Oppenheimer and Richard Feynman, the first lean as a pencil, the other a fine-boned Puck sweetly naughty as that Shakespearean provocateur. Dead men if for the flight from Europe, these outcast performers orchestrated in New Mexico what would be the century's biggest spectacle, to daze and dazzle a darkened world.

The Holocaust and Hiroshima are twin icons of the apocalyptic violence that inaugurates the modern age. At the center of both—like it or not—are Jews. If they were half of the twelve million consigned to death in Europe, Jews comprised an even larger percentage of the scientists whose efforts in New Mexico would transform two Japanese cities, likewise, into ash. Wartime chronicling, like Holocaust memorialization, is typically painted as a series of two-dimensional poster boards to victory and defeat. In one, tragedy: the "black milk" of Célan's "Deathfuge." In the other, courage: the Allied effort to win the weapons race against the Nazis. Insulated from each other and from us, these wartime simulacra offer an appropriately dignified version of World War II history as epic, larger than life, a theater of extraordinary action and heightened emotion.

Jettison these, and we lose the monumental grandeur that retrospectively lends coherence to violence. But we obtain a quality of attention that restores to modern Jewish experience its richness and detail. At a minimum, the knowledge that the relatives of the victims of the gas chambers were instrumental in the race to develop the most potent weapons on Earth should give us pause. In the disparate countenances of these scientists, a range of feeling too mixed to find a place within the exalted rhetoric of wartime contest, an alloy of rage and hope resisting ruin. Juxtapose a photograph of the physicists who worked in Los Alamos side by side with a picture taken through the barbed wire mesh of Auschwitz. In the memorial photograph, breathing stick figures stare back at you. Too emaciated to stand up straight, they still pose for the camera. Their black eyes smolder, guttered fires that will flame up again at the slightest provocation of the air.

Turn to the equally famous image of Albert Einstein, and the accomplishments as well as afflictions of Jewish lives in the twentieth century come into focus. Einstein, his Mona Lisa smile at odds with the sad dark eyes, large and lustrous and fringed with lashes heavy as half-drawn curtains. And then there is the sidelong smile itself, the very icon of Jewish experience, with its marvelous shades of feeling, bittersweet and rueful, lilting as the minor-keyed clarinet melodies of klezmer music, a little melancholy, a little mocking, epigrammatic, knowing. A smile that is ironic and romantic and pragmatic, quizzical without bemusement, nostalgic for a childhood paradise it recognizes it never enjoyed, slightly superior but hesitant (hovering at the corners of the mouth like a watcher at the edges of a party); a flirtatious smile that mutates from seduction to sadness in an instant; a glancing smile with the head turned a quarter turn away from you yet that still engages you steadfastly and squarely with the "*j'accuse*" that neither Jews nor non-Jews would ever mistake for mere abstractedness.

The time has come to return this sidelong look with an equally searching gaze, forgoing the satisfactions of bereavement in order to examine more complicated solutions to the untenable choices history offers. Einstein, we know, refused to become involved in the wartime science that would translate his famous theory into its most destructive practice. But many other Jewish physicists were instrumental in the work the young Feynman saw as necessary, given what he called, with his penchant for understatement, the "fright" of Germany's militarism. Their hearts beating faster in the thin desert air, the physicists who gathered at Los Alamos waved away mourning, forgoing Kaddish as they bent their heads together in the race to solve each day's scientific problems. The clamor of the lab's cafeteria refused the myth of silence, Europe's slow procession of shades packing their bags to hell without sound or sigh. The mathematical language these physicists spoke was competitive, argumentative, barely containable at presto tempo.

At Norway's Norsk Hydro plant, Nazi engineers oversaw the stepped-up production of heavy water—water laced with deuterium, the hydrogen isotope whose denser molecular structure releases neutrons that moderate and control the reactions that split uranium atoms. Learning of this effort from a Dutch colleague who had been expelled from the Kaiser Wilhelm Institute, Einstein wrote a letter of warning to Roosevelt. The president did not immediately pay attention to this resident "alien" of whom the FBI pronounced in the early 1940s: "This office would not recommend the employment of Dr. Einstein, on matters of a secret nature, without a very careful investigation, as it seems unlikely that a man of his background could, in such a short time, become a loyal American citizen."

In the end, many scientists "of his background"—socialists and Jews—were invited to collaborate upon the New Mexican–based bomb project administrated by Robert J. Oppenheimer, himself blacklisted after the war. In an irony we would do well to acknowledge, it was the refugee from Hungary, Edward Teller, who later spoke most vociferously against this young American. Oppenheimer gave twenty hours of each day and some thirty pounds on an already too-slender frame to the Manhattan Project. Still, in 1954, he was essentially "tried" for disloyalty, his security clearances permanently revoked, his legacy ineradicably blackened. His wife, Kitty, had once been married to Joseph Dallet, a member of the Communist Party who had been killed in 1937 while fighting for the Republican side during the Spanish Civil War. This "affiliation"—if such it was, for when does your partner's former spouse become your own relative?—was sufficient to scapegoat Oppenheimer.

In the early 1940s, however, the tensions between the impolitic Jewish refugee and the urbane scion of a wealthy Jewish American family were shoved aside. The escaped scientists who occupied side-by-side offices at Los Alamos had been spat at and despised by Europe. Above deep Atlantic seas, from the decks of the ocean liners, they watched home recede beyond the horizon line. But not beyond memory. Reviled by the countries that would forever remain their native lands, is it any wonder they chose an affiliation that made more respectful use of their intellectual gifts?

In New Mexico they substituted cooperation and what Feynman condescendingly labeled "engineering" in place of the pure science that gave to their lives its rare and sustaining grace. Like other brilliant people fortunate enough to find outlets for self-expression in their work, these physicists possessed the ability to become so wholly absorbed in concentration that the separate antiphonies of self resolved momentarily into a single clear note. Such intellectual joy they sacrificed, for a time, at Los Alamos: shelving the questions and musings that surfaced at odd moments of the day to remind them of their real interests, so that they could, committee-like, construct a bomb. But for the refugees, particularly, I suspect that a certain degree of camaraderie—the fellowship they had once enjoyed in their own European laboratories until it became unalterably compromised in the early 1930s—compensated for the temporary cessation of their larger concerns. Much scholarly collaboration is an uneasy mix of people in suspension rather than solution. The scientists at Los Alamos—with their inside jokes and their Sunday walks in the canyons, their summer camp dormitory arrangements and their weekend parties— were fiercely competitive as only the intellectually self-possessed can be, but they were united in their common aim, their respect for one another's work, even, paradoxically, their maverick iconoclasm.

Those of us born decades after World War II have been raised in the long shadow of nuclear fallout. We know apocalypse as unpleasant fact, a slow toxicity: radiation deposited in our bones from yearly X-rays, the painstaking accretion of mercury in our blood, the thickening and blurring of our atmosphere with carcinogenic fuel emissions so that we no longer see the horizon of clear days. Of course the scientists gathered in Los Alamos during wartime would have preferred pursuing their own work: questions about the formation of the stars, the as-yet-unnamed forces far more potent than gravity that seemed to be keeping whole constellations from collapsing, the origin of the universe itself. These large, ennobling problems had occupied them before the petty but virulent spite of human conflicts redirected their collective intelligences toward the service of weaponry. For them, apocalypse was imminent.

The silence from their families overseas would have sounded loud as the hiss of a blank tape. Worry about their welfare would have clouded their focus and destroyed their concentration, so that they must have been grateful to be occupied. Late in the war, reports of barracks constructed with the sole object of dispatching those they housed to oblivion had begun to circulate in the classified circles many of the scientists were privy to. In these shadowy death cities that had sprung up on the edges of ordinary towns, clocks marked the hours from waking to work to extinction in grotesque imitation of quotidian rhythms.

How strange to wake to this purity of sun and light in New Mexico instead, the blue dome of sky contoured by clouds, the piñon and scrub pines falling away on the slopes below you, the peaks of the Jemez range on the far horizon deepening the clear expanse till it appears profound as the space between stars. Los Alamos offered the long view, the mesas slow to crumble, the half-lives of stones carved by wind and the endless cycle of sunlight a geologic measure that reduced all the grandeur and grimness of the last five hundred years of European history to a second's shadow across the sun. No wonder Oppenheimer chose this place, the same one he had ridden across so often as a young man with the few companions strong enough to weather his fourteen-hour stretches on horseback. On the weekends, the scientists hiked with him up the rock faces of the mesas surrounding their temporary quarters and steadied their palms against the sun-warmed contours of stone. Breathing hard in the thin air, did they see the dark mirages of their families waver on the horizon?

At a minimum, they must have felt the adrenaline surge of satisfaction when they manipulated a power immeasurably more concentrated than the chemicals made by German companies that were vented through "shower-heads" to suffocate the history professor down the street, the neighborhood bully who had tormented a son, the clarinet player next door whose eternal practicing was audible through the walls when traffic ceased. Later, surveying photographs of the lunar rubble of Hiroshima and Nagasaki (empty as the abandoned death camps in Europe that likewise denied the bereaved the consolation of gravestones), did some of them turn their back on the New Mexico skies to face Europe again and whisper—knowing the burden they left in the doorframes of the bombed-out houses—*This is finished in your name?*

"Now I am become Death, the destroyer of worlds." The eulogy J. Robert Oppenheimer pronounced after the bomb detonated has become proverbial for American global dominance. But Oppenheimer's first-person pronoun gestured as well to people across the seas in Italy, Germany, Hungary, and France, binding the refugee scientists in Los Alamos to their separate geographies of home. For the director of the Manhattan Project, there was that other kinship, a tug of recognition slight and uncomfortably familiar as an irregular beat of the heart, which gave to his grave pronouncement a more pointed edge. What more appropriate power for Oppenheimer—cosmopolitan, scholarly, open minded—to call up as epitaph for the Jews of Europe than the spirit of Shiva? Physical principle rather than vengeful deity, the Hindu god appeals equally to the tenets of science and belief. Shiva is entropy. Cosmic assessor of destructive forces, he judges the capacity of systems to tolerate chaos—and so provided Oppenheimer a way to negotiate between physics and faith. Too worldly to be wholeheartedly religious, too wealthy to commit to physics with the single-minded absorption of the refugees and self-made American men he managed, he found in Shiva, however attenuated, the retributive force of his heart.

iv. Science and the Spirit

Skepticism rather than blind compliance with established learning characterizes the rabbinic student's disposition and the scientist's ethos alike. Study requires discipline and labor. But what most sharpens its edge, as rabbi and physician Moses Maimonides counsels in the *Guide for the Perplexed* he penned almost a millennium ago, is independence: the thinker must possess "a mind of his own." In eleventh-century Rabbi Shlomo ben Isaac's foundational commentaries on the Torah and Talmud, such critical inquiry often verges on blasphemy. The pluralistic rationalism of the most sophisticated learning in rabbinic schools dazzles like the facets of a cut gemstone. "There are seventy faces to the Torah," rabbinic saying asserts, which condones as many readings of the Bible. The assumption here—that each person possesses the responsibility to tease out his own interpretation—echoes Feynman, as it echoes my father, as it echoes Einstein's own satisfaction with scientific study.

Jewish scientists are quick to distance themselves from religious orthodoxy, but the intellectual qualities Talmudic scholars value are their own. Though Einstein often distinguished the work of science from the study of religion, he was aware that on one level he was translating his predecessors' desire to decipher the laws of God into the laws of physics. "To be sure," he acknowledges in *The World as I See It*, "it is not the fruits of scientific research that elevate a man and enrich his nature, but the urge to understand the intellectual work, creative or receptive. It would surely be absurd to judge the value of the Talmud, for instance, by its intellectual fruits." It is not scientific application that is valuable, but scientific principle that compels. If the field of study has altered, this primary motive—"the urge to understand"—remains a constant across time.

Both Einstein and the medieval rabbinic commentaries value work more than its outcome. "Measured objectively," the physicist asserts, "what a man can wrest from Truth by passionate striving is utterly infinitesimal. But the striving frees us from the bonds of self." In retrospect we might be tempted to reduce this desire to an effort to shelter the self from the virulence of anti-Semitism rather than to understand it as a disinterested desire for enrichment. In a country that mustered a military composure the more rigid for its late unification—Bismarck's rule was recent history, the Franco-Prussian War concluded merely eight years before Einstein's birth—even the most assimilated German Jews remained objects of suspicion. Yet these intellectuals transformed the short-lived progressivism of the Weimar Republic into the new nation's golden age. Berlin's luminous culture was the product of Arnold Schoenberg and Kurt Weill, Max Reinhardt and Edmund Husserl, Theodor Adorno and Walter Benjamin, Freud and Einstein. Nationalists denied them the emotional comforts of home, but release from social stricture fed their critical intelligence while the refusal of community ties sharpened their skepticism, clearing the way for innovation. The vacuum this creative minority left when they were expelled from cultural and political life in the early thirties fooled few. Asked by the Nazi minister of education whether the University of Göttingen had suffered from the loss of Jewish physicists and mathematicians in the spring of 1933, writer Amos Elon reports in *The Pity of It All*, the distinguished mathematician David Hilbert replied: "Suffered? It hasn't suffered, Herr Minister. It no longer exists."

Einstein himself had lectured at the Kaiser Wilhelm Institute in the twenties amid the jeers of *"Juden raus"* (Jews out) from rioting students. But the gall of self-disgust was foreign to him. The mathematical language he listened to was exponentially more powerful than such inconsequential spite. He did not labor to counter derision with his quick-witted aphorisms; these quips were merely a by-product of his own high-spirited energy. Irrepressibly cheerful, he chose the larger world over the small-minded one. In place of the cowering, downcast gaze, he substituted time looking up at the stars. Because intellectual work requires intense concentration, he knew, it releases us momentarily from the constraints of ego, the small resentments, jealousies, dissatisfactions, and annoyances that becloud perception. The sacred is tied as closely to human effort, properly disciplined and appropriately focused, as to divinity itself, that "wind from God sweeping over the water," as Genesis frames what is external to the material world and human consciousness.

Einstein's need to find a kind of human work that is disinterested (immune, that is, to the distractions of illustration and example) is in essence the desire that motivates the religious to envision an alternative to the imperfect world, one remote but which nonetheless resonates in sympathy with our finer feelings. Metaphysical understanding shares with science an interest in principles. Einstein's longing to achieve scientific clarity echoes the yearning of religious scholars to arrive at insight into the divine. And the physicist's language of prayer is thinking, the muscular contractions that push blood through our arteries and oxygenate the receptive tissues of the brain, the bronchiole tubes that expand and contract with every breath, the dendrites and ganglia that stir with each thought, signals jumping from neuron to neuron in a pattern swift and untraceable as blinking lights in the night sky. With these conduits we work toward an understanding of things outside ourselves. Respiration and inspiration, physics and physic: the medieval clerics knew as well as we that metaphysics was a miracle of breath and pulse, of body and mind working in concert to trace pathways from the patterned millions of nerves and neurons inside to the patterned millions of stars outside. To be a doctor was to be a rabbi, to see how physiology permits philosophy, and how philosophy, in its turn, shadows God.

The medical analogies Maimonides exploits throughout his religious writings reflect this genealogy. The essays of certain contemporary physicians who are as facile with philology as physiology maintain this tradition. Perhaps the desire of people across the world to possess a piece of Einstein's brain after his death need not be cynically dismissed as the voyeurism of the circus sideshow but instead as a form of worship that reflects an appreciation for the kinetic and chemical leaps across synapses not so different from leaps of faith.

Like muscle tissue, which atrophies or increases in girth according to our own determined effort, thinking quickens or slackens in concert with the intellectual demands we make of ourselves. We think in order to approach an understanding of the deepest spiritual questions, Maimonides argued. But the power to speculate is not simply conferred upon the heads of the appropriately pious. Reverence—that quality the Puritan culture of New England associates with piety, with decorum, with an unquestioned obedience to duty—is for Jews connected with desire, not the effort to suffocate it, with intellectual skepticism, not catechism, and with an independence of mind that always, always supersedes collective wisdom. Close to a millennium later, Einstein practiced a similar intellectual faith. He did not give up this faith ever: not when his cautions to the U.S. government about German war efforts resulted in the proliferation of weapons of mass destruction, not when the bomb over Hiroshima stilled the city before the nerve signals registering its brilliant ravaging could make their way to the brains of the watchers, not even when he knew the busy firings inside his own brain were within hours of ceasing. *Cogito, ergo sum.* I think, therefore I am. If Einstein inaugurated the modern scientific age, he was still a child of Descartes. The day he died of a stomach aneurism, he lay in his hospital bed writing out equations.

Jews are often seen as parochial, an irony of epic proportions given the cosmopolitanism of Jewish intellectualism. All over the world, different Jewish cultures take the phrase "intellectual work" seriously. Surprisingly, this education has changed very little over the centuries. If the origins of scholarly inquiry seem insular in the sense that they derive from religious interpretation, take a closer look. The secular among us may ridicule the Talmudic thinker as the original bespectacled nerd, but the study groups within which students cluster spur the kind of bravura academic performance that characterizes the best thinkers.

v. Art, Science, and the Sublime

As a literature professor, I have been schooled to understand tragedy as the apex of achievement. In concert with the opening lines of Tolstoy's *Anna Karenina* ("Happy families are all alike; every unhappy family is unhappy in its own way"), literary critics balk at affirmation. Like Chagall's glorious palette, however, writings by Einstein and Feynman communicate happiness far more often than defeat. And why shouldn't this fugitive, alchemical presence occupy our imaginative lives? If loss is complicated, how much more so the momentary luminescence of joy? While we linger upon sorrow in prose and verse, the vitality of midcentury painters owes much to the sensibilities of their modernist precursors whose energy reanimated the plastic arts. Think of the kinetic dazzle of Jackson Pollock's canvases, where paint pulses with the uncontainable energy of some unstable element. Matisse's warmly lit abstractions of the French landscape. Picasso's canon—imperial, muscular, assertive—and save for *Guernica*, a refusal of the darkness of war. And then there are the Jewish painters: the protomodern light experiments of Camille Pisarro and Max Lieberman. Mark Rothko's shimmering rectangles, lucent as the surface of water. The figures in Chagall's canvases that hover midway between earth and sky to mirror the elusive and inexplicable rise of the spirits.

The paintings of this Russian immigrant harbor ghosts less often than they beckon toward the dancing of circus performers. Canvases glow bright as crayon boxes. Color is so vibrant here it seems the point of painting: the blue of the azure, greens piquant as unfurling leaves, reds the cheerful crimson of newly oxygenated blood. Despite the disparagement of some native-born French, Moische Segal, survivor of pogrom and Holocaust and newly naturalized citizen, adorned the ceiling of the new Paris Opera with the effulgent hues of Tintoretto. Color—tender as spring, high-spirited as children at Purim, glamorous as Mardi Gras or the kinetic streak of red and white traffic light on time-exposed photographic films—speaks in the accents of joy in almost all of Chagall's work.

Of course the painter was as intimate with loss as with the Torah stories he translated to paint. But sorrow he mostly contained. Melancholy remained part of the past, visible in the faint smile—a not-so-distant mirror to Einstein's own—that played across his father's lips. "Everything about my father seemed enigma and sadness to me," Chagall writes in *My Life*, his autobiography. "Always tired, careworn, only his eyes had a luster, of grey-blue. . . . He lifted heavy barrels [of herring], and my heart ached to see him hoist those loads, his frozen hands fumbling. . . . Only his face occasionally betrayed a faint smile. What a smile! Where did it come from?" Like Einstein, whose unfathomable smile simultaneously opens to and answers for sadness, Chagall recognizes melancholy only to confine it to the horizon line of his Russian homeland.

The refugee's wisdom: we can never recover, unless we finally stop listening.

And so, sadness shimmers faintly in the blue tones that outline the artist's peasant homes and faraway cathedral bell. But the present is full of work, the satisfying soulful work of painting, where happy scenes are squarely foregrounded. Light, color, movement—there is the Eiffel Tower, here the chatter of talk and the clink of glassware along Paris's tree-lined avenues. Lovers float above the ground like bright balloons escaping, fiddlers chase away death playing on rooftops above town streets, the petals of flowers glisten like stars.

If we were to express feeling in the language of physics, then happiness would be kinetic as the artist's softly wavering canvases. Sorrow is absolute zero, the absence of energy, when even the hummingbird vibration of atoms quivers into stillness. Gladness trembles like the dappled light in Chagall's circus pictures, which defy grief as they defy Newton's laws. Dancers pirouette in air while a clown clasps a donkey round the waist. Human and animal alike glow with the green-yellow tones of spring.

The painter understands color the way a physicist interprets the spectrum. Not as pigment or hue but as energy, the dynamic freight of each picture's mood and argument. Stand in front of one of Chagall's stained-glass windows and you cannot fail to understand this force. "Just materials and light," he explained, and "something mystical passes through the window." Beauty drove Einstein too. Nor was this aesthetic impulse idiosyncratic; mathematicians will tell you that the finest expressions possess their own spare grace. The most elegant algebraic solution is the simplest. Shorn of unnecessary parts, the letters, symbols, and numbers vibrate with the suppressed energy of Kandinsky's neon canvases. Stripping a mathematical phrase to its fewest elements is profoundly satisfying. In its cogency, its harmonious containment of affiliation and design, it gestures toward what Einstein and other physicists knew was an infinitely interconnected universe. William Carlos Williams echoes this idea in "The Rose" when he imagines a flower petal and the world its curved edge defines. "From the petal's edge a line starts / that being of steel / infinitely fine, infinitely / rigid penetrates / the Milky Way / without contact." Crafted in language as transparent as the meeting of rose and atmosphere it perceives, the poet's understanding of the "fragility of the flower / unbruised" as it "penetrates space" is also Einstein's belief in the comprehension of reality as spelled out in the unifying terms of general relativity. "If uniform motion was relative," the physicist assumed, then "*all* motion should be." This aesthetic dissatisfaction—an unhappiness with special relativity because it was "ugly"—moved Einstein to formulate what the editors of his writings in *The Human Side* call with sympathetic understanding "gravitational equations of transcendent beauty."

Chagall's calculus expressed art as the sum of materials and light. Einstein's greatest insight about the relationship of mass and energy originated from a similar focus on the natural world's basic elements and a corresponding faith in its unity. Earth's balance is everywhere reflected: in the tensile strength of a single hair and in the perfect proportions of an Ionic column, whose flower-stem slenderness holds thousands of pounds of marble aloft. The physicist's most famous equation expresses with austere beauty the "profound interrelationships" that compose our world. Einstein's equation is a mathematical metaphor for an elegant universe regulated from interstellar space to single-celled organism by the same physical principles. Marvelously efficient on the page, it gestures toward forces of such magnitude most of us cannot conceptualize them without the aid of analogy. "E," "c," "m," the number "2": the alphabet a child learns. $E=mc^2$, symbols connecting immensities with minutiae. To contemplate this equation is to see the microcosm in the world and the universe contained in a grain of sand. Travel far enough away from the blue-green radiance of Earth and this small round beauty becomes the colored iris of a human eye. Even as dark energy scatters stars, cohesion rounds a water droplet into a globe.

The writings of scientists reflect the same affectionate awe for the world that is visible in Chagall's buoyant canvases. We are quick to understand twentieth-century physics as our era's heart of darkness, but this is to mistake its crudest physical expression, the technological power unleashed during warfare, for its supreme translation on Earth. The scientists whose investigations with atomic fission led to the engineering of the world's most powerful weapon spent the majority of their lives marveling at a universe whose incomparable beauty was expressed in forces held in harmony, supple and strong and lovely as the sinew from ankle to knee. Reducing the laws of nature to their most elemental relationships was a kind of distillation process, rendering observation free of blur, of noise, of distraction. Einstein's elegant equations were elixir: when he transcribed natural laws into mathematical symbols, he was, like the Greek philosophers, sifting out impurities. Physics was for him a way of listening intently to the music of the spheres. The ancients described the starry skies as suspended in ether, an atmosphere so rarified the world could not breathe it. And physics was to the cosmos what the listening ear was to music: the means by which we connect with what surrounds us in a wholly unmediated way. Direct as touch, sufficient in itself, this is an insight too fine to be carried by language. Its equations link art and nature. Concordance, harmony, balance: this is what Einstein sees in the universe and what a cellist hears in Bach's fugues. Listening, we sum up the balanced frequencies of each note into purity in our ear. Like the cello's spare loveliness, Einstein's equation possesses infinite expressive power.

Function creates form. Understanding the intricate design that holds forces balanced in tension is an aesthetic and an ethic, providing artistic and scientific observations with their profound depth. Einstein gestures toward this sense of connection in his 1931 travel diary, writing of a winter storm: "The sea has a look of indescribable grandeur, especially when the sun falls on it. One feels as if one is dissolved and merged into Nature. Even more than usual, one feels the insignificance of the individual, and it makes one happy." How many of us have felt the sharpness of our own losses gentled when we look out over the expanse of ocean or the dome of sky, knowing the endless waves of water and wind and cloud across horizons will remain long after our own hearts have stopped? The grandeur that Einstein felt at the water's edge mirrors the sublime insight Genesis offers: "The earth being unformed and void, with darkness over the surface of the deep and a wind from God sweeping over the water." Light generates itself from chaos. Just so, the recognition of a being dissolved and released of the weight of significance in a greater power brings ease and lightness. Creation does not issue from bitterness or a sense of affliction but rather from grateful understanding of the poised, interrelated forces at work in the world's design.

vi. Beyond Descartes: Doubt as Invention

The brilliantly energetic skepticism that characterizes the work of Jewish physicists is as much the hallmark of Jewish culture as is the piety of melancholy. To doubt is not to falter or despair. It is to create possibility, to see the world in a different way, to sweep away established wisdom without a second thought or second look when that legacy does not adequately explain experience. The blind reverence to memory and stubborn hold on the past long attributed to Jews are merely by-products of this unhesitating energy, an after-the-fact apology compensating for a defiance that catalyzes innovation. In a postwar lecture on "The Value of Science" delivered at the 1955 meeting of the National Academy of Sciences, Feynman privileged skepticism when he defined scientific knowledge as a collection of statements of "varying degrees of certainty—some most unsure, some nearly sure, but none absolutely certain." Incertitude catalyzes exploration. The "freedom to doubt" is a liberty—a privilege wrested "out of a struggle against authority in the early days of science." Permit us to question, these seventeenth-century thinkers demanded. Allow us "to not be sure," the twentieth-century researcher repeats.

Asking questions, not supplying ready answers, makes good science. Here we come full circle, to the traditions of study explained by Shlomo ben Isaac and Maimonides, traditions sustained by Talmudic study to this day. In *"What Do You Care What Other People Think?"* Feynman recalls a discussion of electricity he led for a class of rabbinical students in New York City. He assumed, with his usual arrogance, that science would best their religious logic. But they were ten times quicker than he was. "As soon as they saw I could put them in a hole, they went twist, turn, twist—I can't remember how—and they were free! I thought I had come up with an original idea—phooey! It had been discussed in the Talmud for ages!" Here is the Jew as escape artist, the intellectual Houdini who wriggles free of his chains and slips out of confinement, the wartime refugee who eludes the Shoah with the light-footedness a starvation diet allows. In the midst of gloom, the lilt of klezmer music, an alto clarinet kicking up its heels like a wedding dancer. A hint of melancholy in the minor key played at allegro tempo. And always ideas, intellectual fission released as marvelous, uncontainable energy.

Then there is Feynman himself, an imp who writes of his safecracking and lockpicking tricks in "Surely You're Joking, Mr. Feynman!" with uncontainable glee. In the iron-clad security of Los Alamos, the scientist is a human dust devil blowing away other scientists before his antics like tumbleweeds in fright:

> I went back to the first filing cabinet and CLICK! It opened! . . . Now *I* could write a safecracker book that would beat every one. . . . I opened safes whose contents were . . . more valuable than what any safecracker anywhere had opened—except for a life, of course. . . . The safes which contained all the secrets to the atomic bomb: the schedules for the production of the plutonium, the purification procedures, how much material is needed, how the bomb works, how the neutrons are generated, what the design is, the dimensions—the entire information that was known at Los Alamos: *the whole schmeer!*

At the heart of darkness this sprite, exposing security flaws and defying gravitas, sidestepping sermon, mocking seriousness, delighting in his own brilliance with a childlike openness that deflates any claim to destructive self-importance. To observe the slight figure of the physicist watch his colleague blanch before a safe that is empty save for a scrap of paper scrawled in red crayon with the words "Feynman was here" is to witness that other Jewish tradition, an energy that flaunts grief to find a trickster's happiness at the center of gloom.

Much scientific brilliance was volunteered at Los Alamos in service of weapons that remain the vanishing point for our own nightmares. But death, destruction, and the world laid waste need not be the end of the story. The same wartime refugees—outsiders like Albert Einstein, Wolfgang Pauli, and Emilio Segrè—have given the Earth its location among the stars, explored galaxies at the outer edge of the universe, discovered the forces that keep the void of space from collapsing in upon itself, else no Earth, no sun, no stars, no universe. Why see the faces of Jewish people as the fallen leaves of history, scuttling this way and that according to an ill-intentioned German wind? At the very period memorialized by history as a dead loss, an era of unspeakable suffering whose end point is a mass vanishing, Jews remade the cosmos. The nadir of Jewish history marks the greatest profusion of scientific ideas since Newton, and these physicists, pushed malignly to the edges and then out of sight of Europe altogether, were central to its flourishing.

The omniscient grandeur earlier centuries gave to the angels, the scientists bestowed on themselves—not as creators, but with the humility of intelligent watchers. They contemplated the beginnings of time and its end, watched as stars exploded, imploded, and exploded again, their materials coming to momentary rest in the iron of our blood and bones. Not passive, not waiting, not paralyzed by despair, the people pushed to the margins of their own townships traveled out to expand boundaries most of us could not even invent, much less understand. The destructive energy that found a language in the barked commands of midcentury wartime was nothing to these scientists' positively charged masses, volatile with ideas, exuberant with the momentum of insights they knew were inescapable, unstoppable, transforming.

I could not understand even the simplest physics equation to save my life, but the cocky insouciance for "what other people will say" conforms closely to my familial experience. I recognize in Feynman's inimitable self-possession an ebullience akin to my father's brashness, as well as an impatience with the social rituals of the less curious who took refuge in site visits and committee meetings while he wanted only to be in the lab, thinking. Intellectual tendentiousness and a sublime lack of fear at jettisoning accepted wisdom is my inheritance too—albeit in a different academic environment than the research medicine that is my father's profession or the theoretical physics that is the province of so many Jewish scientists.

So, writer and reader of literature that I am, I stumble through Brian Greene's *Elegant Universe* hoping in my snail's pace to pick up a few surface understandings about string theory and edge my way through the tangled thicket of *The Fabric Of the Cosmos* anticipating that a few small burrs of insight about our eleven-dimensional world will stubbornly cling to my sleeve. I know that this very desire to learn is in my case a provocation inherited as well as discovered, a cultural impulse pleasing and profound as the muscular intelligence that performs its own daily miracles when we lift a cup to our lips, or draw a violin bow across a string, or, like my artist daughter Zoë, put pen to paper. I have neither studied Talmud nor sat for more than two hours at a time listening to rabbinical sermons. But it is to thousands of years of these scholarly traditions that my own pleasure in learning in part originates. Effortless as the body's memory, and as poised, the gift of intellectual brashness opens to a kind of secular faith. The math may be performed by supercomputers in windowless laboratories, but still, it is stargazing that catalyzes such scientific inquiry. What more spiritual than this, this unbalancing looking up at the dome of sky, your hands raised slightly to compensate for your body's tilting, your head thrown back—this open-throated but unspeakable yearning, this willingness to connect to what is beyond the self that ends in rapturous acceptance of the world's mystery? Here, the past is not a burden, nor a bitterness without balm. Instead, it curves toward the future; just as, looking up, we think beyond our present moment illuminated by starlight from places gone before all of us—nation after nation, people after people—began, slow as a flower's unfurling, to move from the crouch of four feet to learn the upright stance that makes stargazing possible.

What more curious gift than the capacity we have of bending time, the way a few moments recalled in the lightning flashes of memory obliterate the darkness of difficult years? Such refugee scientists show us that against humanity's timeless cruelty—ancient "problems from hell" translated into modern genocide—we also possess some understanding of relativity as an interest beyond our own footing. Intellectual work can move equally toward serenity as tragedy. What drives insight is not the pain of loss but a transporting recognition that is outside of the body altogether, outside of humanness, even—a floating upward heedless of gravity that connects us with what the Greeks called the ether and what we still do not know to name.

Science and art extend themselves hopefully as Chagall's lovers, connected by the hands as they leave the ground. And time is the key. Perhaps this is what occupies Jewish physicists in their exploration of the universe: a means to recapture a sense of time as marvel, stretching behind us and in front of us like the seas upon which continents float. In place of the Holocaust, engulfing light and air, they listened for a wind over the darkness that portends movement, a stir of atmosphere that gestures toward presence, a quickening from absence. This conception is ancient and again modern, and no more miraculous than the idea that our own universe—anchored where? And floating in what, if not more space?—will itself grow to fullness to the edges of time, then contract all time back into itself . . . a trillion trillion measures slower, yes, than the memory of human life—but sure as the rhythmic rise and fall of our own breathing.

LEAVING RUSSIA

The Soulful Modernism of Chagall and Rothko

As the sun rose upon the earth and Lot entered Zoar, the Lord rained upon Sodom and Gomorrah sulfurous fire from the Lord out of heaven. He annihilated those cities and the entire Plain, and all the inhabitants of the cities and the vegetation of the ground. Lot's wife looked back, and she thereupon turned into a pillar of salt.

Next morning, Abraham hurried to the place where he had stood before the Lord, and, looking down toward Sodom and Gomorrah and all the land of the Plain, he saw the smoke of the land rising like the smoke of a kiln.

—Genesis 19:23–28

1. Antecedents

Genesis frames the destruction of Sodom and Gomorrah in language so matter of fact it could be meteorological account, not story. Apocalypse requires only a sentence: in the time it takes to blink dust from your eye, the city is gone. A few more words and Lot's wife has disappeared. Abraham looks back at the dead land through air that still quivers with heat, but the writers of Genesis do not spare a heartbeat to mourn the woman's passing.

The absence of commemoration may be memorial's purest form but vanishing haunts like neglect. In the Greek narratives that precede Judaism, renewal tempers dissolution. Roses bloom when Persephone rejoins Demeter every summer. The lilt of Orpheus's lyre calls back Eurydice. In lines of verse that stretch over story the way tendon slides over bone, Ovid, a Roman poet, reshapes the halfway human into beautiful form. Extinction translates into alchemy as a torso stiffens into a tree trunk and the glint of blonde hair trembles amid flickering leaves.

The destruction of Lot's wife, for obvious reasons, involves no such sensuality. There is metamorphosis here, but nothing transformative. Obliterated for a backward glance, Lot's wife is permitted neither reprieve nor the solace of sorrow. Homesickness for a distempered place destroys her and then God annihilates her memory. Old Testament punishment boasts an elegant symmetry: the woman who refuses to leave without regret is fused to the place where she took her last look. The lines of prose do not deny feeling; they vaporize it. The soft skin of Idit's upper thigh, the warmth of her breath, the pulse beating fast in her throat and temple: all harden at once to mineral. The tears that dry into a pillar of salt offer merely a stone's grief.

This economy of expression is almost unintelligible in the context of contemporary effusiveness. Our public performances of desolation, as of delight, are closer to Greek catharsis than to Judaism's spare aesthetic. The art we create is about display, not concealment; about open-throated mourning, not a blank misery beyond sight and sound. Nonetheless, there is something terrifying about the vacancy Abraham witnesses, this still world lacking any movement but the smoke rising from scorched earth. Its emptiness is absolute, refusing even to harbor grief for what is no longer there: the children squatting in a shady corner, playing house with sticks; the woman intent on scrubbing the dirty hem of a dress; the red-faced baker heaving a tray of loaves from an oven. As if bowing their heads before God's disciplining fire, the writers of Genesis do not testify to the remains of human presence. They give us only blackened earth, the smell of fire, and silence.

Old Testament narrative takes the way of blind prophets who have no need for eyes. Its stories require inward listening, not watchfulness. More often than not they hinge upon refusal, or deprivation. Grief evaporates with incinerated bodies. Sulfur leaches color from fire and rain blunts its heat. As readers we are hostage to this writing, refused sight, hearing, and speech. Perhaps an acrid odor hovers, but we must infer its trace from lines too gaunt to offer sensual evocation. The seared air tastes like gunmetal on the tongue. Salt and sulfur: the materials of a star, or the primeval earth.

Such is Jewish artistry with language. The writing is as starkly beautiful as the desert landscapes upon which its authors lived and died. Yet by nature its aesthetic is one hostile to visual representation. What images could illustrate the instantaneous death of Lot's wife? What palette could color the void? The story of Sodom and Gomorrah enacts the prohibition against image making as unequivocally as the story of the golden calf. Paradoxically, the simile that provides this account of destruction with its solitary embellishment transforms hearths into funeral pyres.

11. Paintings

Fast forward to another apocalypse, several millennia later. In 1919, a bomb whistles through the atmosphere of a German town in the early morning silence. In seconds, the village becomes a volcano. Fragments of metal, flesh, and glass fuse and rain down on Earth. Fire scours the detritus clean. In France, 7 percent of the population leaves for the front lines and does not return. Gas masks spare some firstborn sons in Europe's trenches, but many are not passed over: years later, their dreams of blood and smoke will throttle them nightly. The plague worms its way into Spain only to smite twenty million worldwide. And in Russia? The empire murders its people, and the people turn upon the empire. This is the spectacle of revolution: bayonets stab their way through crowds in Red Square, knives slash tapestries off the walls of country estates, filthy arms sweep gold dishes to the floor in the Winter Palace, tearing the place apart as if it were a used stage set. In a basement room in the city of Ekaterinburg at two o'clock one morning, Nicholas II, a confused Caesar, speaks his final, undignified words—"What? What?"—before being executed, as luck would have it, by a Jewish member of Lenin's secret police. In the streets, Reds and Whites tear flesh from flesh. In the country, Lenin's guards tear up houses and farms looking for grain. And in the villages and towns where Jews live in the Pale of Settlement, the anti-Semitism that permeates the Russian air grows immediately more toxic. "The chosen people of the Bolsheviks," sneers one White officer, as historian Orlando Figes documents in *A People's Tragedy*. Calls for retribution like this transform sporadic pogroms into systemic slaughter.

Two decades after the fields were cleared of bodies and the rutted earth furred over with grass, Mark Rothko began to recall the silent wastes. To my mind, no one more closely approximates the Old Testament despair of modern devastation than this painter. His Seagram murals, a series of orange verticals rising up from black, evoke the spare altars of the ancients. These charred-seeming canvases are the kiln of tragedy, suggesting sacrifice.

Dramatic in their bleakness, they are suffused with awe. The panels the painter arranged several years later in Houston recall the quiet after destruction. Under the light filtering in from the ceiling, the almost indiscernible gradations of blue-black in the canvases that make up the Rothko chapel evoke a quality of empathy more profound than that engineered by a Holocaust museum or war memorial.

The Dvinsk-born artist's earlier works, rendered in more forgiving tones, diffuse an equally mesmerizing brightness. I have sat before the crimson and indigo rectangles of *Number 14, 1960* in San Francisco's Museum of Modern Art more times than I can count. Rothko overpainted this canvas with several washes and the forms shimmering upon its surface seem to float. As I contemplate the painting, the indeterminate edges of these shapes expand until they absorb my field of vision. The smaller blue rectangle rests on the bottom of the canvas as if it were a boat moored in quiet water. Over it, the red hovers like darkening air. The painting invites and rebuffs entrance simultaneously, the way the line between sea and sky draws you near at the same time that it estranges you from its grandeur. The black hue bordering and dividing these colored forms blurs in and out of my sight. Its charcoal color feels as external as the darkness of space and as intimate as the mind-darkness from which memory's images surface.

Rothko makes apocalypse understandable by investing it with human feeling. Marc Chagall, a painter born sixteen years earlier in Vitebsk, imagines Eden to recall us to rapture. Though he endured the Russian Revolution and the First World War and then dodged the Holocaust as a refugee, he continued to paint delight. To stand in front of his canvases is to be bathed in color resplendent as stained glass. In the face of sorrow (the loss of his wife, Bella, the loss of his country, the losses suffered by his people), Chagall's paintings are joyous folktales whose lively compositions dance to the unheard cadences of klezmer. In *The Promenade* (1917), *Birthday* (1915), and *Over the Village* (1914–18), tributes to Bella he painted in the first years of their marriage, secular history bows to sacred time. In place of blood-rust, the burnt umber of charred buildings, and the washed-out sepia of war, Chagall selects softly brilliant hues: rose, violet, celestial blue. Color defies the monochrome of waste. The buoyant space of his paintings floats viewers upward: away from the front, the operating table, the nighttime breadlines lengthening and lengthening in the subzero streets.

The tension in Rothko's paintings reminds you that you hold yourself upright in defiance of Earth's gravity. Chagall makes you weightless. The figures in his canvases are often poised halfway between ground and atmosphere; watching them, it is easy to imagine your own hold relinquished. To look at the canvases is to drift through the skies above Vitebsk, to fly alongside the Eiffel Tower or to soar toward the ceiling of the Opéra Garnier in a dream of Paris, a visual aria no less lovely than the voices rising up from the stage.

In the language of space Chagall finds a way to figure time so that the high-flown perspectives of the canvases carry us far away from the present. Choosing to adopt the tender but distant gaze of the angels who hover in his paintings, he creates in his viewers a sense of distracted affiliation toward the proceedings that unfold in front of them. Fragments of feeling—love, tenderness, joy—rise upward like the thoughts the celestial onlookers in Wim Wender's *Wings of Desire* overhear as they linger above a girl folding shirts in a clothing store and a small boy reading in his room. Chagall's gaze is equally a benediction, a hand placed lightly on the forehead of the sleeper to soothe a restless mind. War, famine, the bile of revenge—this too will pass, the canvases seem to say.

In *The Promenade*, finished during the tumultuous period of the 1917 Revolution, Chagall makes Russia green again. The artist and his wife are in the foreground. The outlines of the city of Vitebsk, painted the color of fat summer leaves, create a low horizon. Debonair as a musician in a black tux, the young Chagall stands facing us. He is smiling. One foot rests upon the edge of a ruby-colored picnic cloth decorated with flowers, where a carafe and a glass of wine also sit. In his right hand, the artist holds a bird. His left, extended heavenward, clasps Bella's hand as if her palm were the string of a balloon. Fuchsia-colored, serene, she floats above him, her body inclined in parallel with the emerald earth. The opaque sky is tenderer than the jade benediction of grass and houses, gentler than the coral church dome whose soft color Bella's dress curiously echoes. Lovely as a pearl, lovely as Bella, this luminous atmosphere makes your own heart rise.

I look at this painting of lovers with my own by my side and feel a transient joy. Happinesses of the present and past mingle, and there is the sweetness of surfeit. It is a moment in which the intangibilities of feeling are too fine for speech. Chagall's sky glows with a faint opalescence, like snow reflecting the colored light of sunset. The wash of tones evokes recollections as finely graded. The thin clear air of New Mexico at dusk. The smell of rain from an open door. The sound of wood beams creaking as a house cools in the darkness. For a moment, my separate selves merge. In the same instant I become aware of their different existences, they are reconciled.

What do we really see when we look at a painting such as *The Promenade*? Is it memory that enriches painting? Or something in the canvas that restores recollection? We assume that the power visual artists hold rests in their ability to provoke us by seeing differently—by making things strange. Not so. The new might turn our heads, but something deeper keeps us looking, something that resonates with our own visual fields, horizon lines sustained as much from the insight of memory as from sight itself. If a painting works, it haunts us until what we assumed existed outside of us becomes part of ourselves. Art reconciles the blurry silhouettes of memory that shadow us as we stand in the noon sun of the present. Its design offers us a way to discipline the fragments of our past that surface at random—a picnic overlooking the olive slopes of falling away hills outside the Santa Fe opera, the salmon-colored tie a brother wore to his medical school graduation, the cantilevered struts of the Eiffel Tower's steps you climbed with a daughter one afternoon. In this way, looking at a painting can be a way to understand, as Hemingway writes in *A Moveable Feast*, how time can both go "very slowly" and "all at once."

I stare at this work and wonder what visual grammar enables its arrangement of color and form to speak to me, while a nearby painting composed like this one from a pattern of shapes and hues remains inert. A curious chemistry animates the layers of pigment on canvas. Just as a recollected image brings back time and place, trespassing every means by which we understand the world outside ourselves, so the eye that regards this painting ushers in all five senses. Its frame blurs into the grainy diffuseness of my peripheral vision and I realize that I am no longer seeing as much as thinking, hearing, recollecting. Like much of Chagall's best work, this painting returns me to the past as the canvas opens before my eyes in the moment. In place of the modern wasteland of the Russian Revolution and World War I, a second that refuses to tick past, the Vitebsk artist substitutes an instant of love whose fullness compensates for its transience: quantity stretched to its limit. The two linked figures shimmer on the canvas like midsummer, like a dragonfly glimpsed before its iridescence darts past your eye, like the dome of sky on a day "serene from the start, almost painfully slowed" as Stanley Kunitz offers in his translation of Osip Mandelstam's poem "Summer Solstice."

As with Rothko's Seagram murals, Chagall's *The Promenade* does not exact a distancing admiration. Instead, its intimacy enraptures. Neither painter possessed Picasso's virtuoso technique or angry energy, but the canvases of both Rothko and Chagall provoke an expressive response the Spanish innovator rarely elicits. Gaze at one of his works, and you are reminded none too gently of the chasm that separates you from this virtuoso. Chagall's energy, like Rothko's, is entirely directed toward communication. How unlike the fracturing, fragmenting canvases of modernism, their invitation to reflection. Cubism shatters the complacencies of vision only to offer us the jagged sightlines of competing perspectives. Rothko and Chagall provide completion, not division. You look at them not to see the world but to know yourself.

III. Predecessors

What does it mean to dedicate your life's energy to what is considered impossible, a blasphemy, a contradiction in terms? To be a Jewish painter in Russia at the turn of the century was to cast off the religious strictures of familial embrace and to defy the legal prohibitions that denied Jews the liberties other Russian citizens enjoyed: the freedom to own land, to attend public school, to live in the city or town of your own choosing. And yet both Marc Chagall and Mark Rothko remained obdurately committed to visual expression in a culture and a country united perhaps only in this, its refusal to permit any such authority. The Vitebsk native was cheerful, energetic, and gregarious despite his constant impatience with the social life that stole painting time. The youth from Dvinsk was the mirror of melancholy, an urbane but solitary person who walked the night streets of New York City as if he had stepped out of an Edward Hopper canvas. Both Chagall and Rothko were iconoclasts driven to learn a visual idiom no one around them cared to speak. The early years saw them devoted to a profession so little enamored it did not muster the energy sufficient to ostracize them. But at their deaths they left behind the canvases familiar to us on the walls of the world's most distinguished museums.

In the decades before Chagall and Rothko began painting, few Jewish artists came to prominence in Russia. Only a scattering attended the illustrious St. Petersburg Imperial Academy of Art and its more progressive counterpart, the Moscow School. But Russia's relentless anti-Semitism did not wholly prevent exceptional painters from thriving. When Isaak Levitan died in 1900 from a bad heart at forty, he left Russia his evocative renderings of its countryside. His success might have been prompted by Anton Chekhov, who vigorously championed him and with whom he was inseparable at twenty. Maybe it was simply Levitan's studiedly pastoral repertoire that appealed. Or perhaps this artist's celebrity was ensured by the patronage of Sergei Treyakov, the businessman who founded the distinguished gallery that bears his name in Moscow. Regardless, though poor and Jewish, Levitan became, by the age of thirty-five, one of Russia's most renowned painters.

Two decades before Chagall honored his family's faith in portraits such as *The Rabbi* (1922) and *Jew with Torah* (1925), Levitan promoted landscape painting, a genre just developing in Russia, which usually equated rural iconography with nationalism. Weathered roofs of village houses, lakes darkened with cloud cover, plains golden with stubble or the new green of May: this was the artist's repertoire—lovely, distinctively Russian, disarmingly rustic for a Moscow orphan. That Levitan's paintings conspicuously lacked any reference to Judaism hardly hindered his growing fame. Whether his project was self-negating remains an open question, despite the anecdote critic Averil King offers in *Isaak Levitan: Lyrical Landscape*. As the artist painted with colleague Konstantin Vysotsky by the banks of the Volga, church bells sounded in the distance. Not "ostentatiously, but deliberately enough" for his companion to observe, the Jewish painter made the sign of the cross. Was the gesture devout? A dissembling for safety's sake? Or did Levitan simply wish to acknowledge the other's faith in the reverence of a deepening twilight?

Studying *Vladimirka Road* (1892) in London's National Gallery, where it was on view during an exhibition of nineteenth-century Russian painting, afforded me no definitive answers. This large canvas is beautiful and oppressive. Grasses blow in the foreground, but winter is incipient in the scudding clouds overhead. Vladimirka was an infamous route, the path trod by dissidents, many of them Jewish, as they marched in shackles toward the labor camps of Siberia. The contrast between the land's verdancy and the dark sky, then, speaks more than seasonal melancholy. The leisurely movement of fall toward the dark season ahead would have been nothing to the creeping passage of years these prisoners faced. Contemplating this painting, I could not help but see its dirt track as the artist's way of gesturing toward such painful extension. The road stretches monotonously across the canvas toward an inscrutable end on the horizon. Here a tiny black-clothed woman stands solitary, the small vertical of a wayside altar her only measure.

Above Eternal Rest (1894), the painter's own favorite work, re-creates not just altar but church entire. Here, too, the gesture toward Christianity in the canvas remains unreadable. Taking their cue from its title, most Russian accounts of this painting ignore the preposition and reduce the work's tension to the pull between life and death. (But then they also refuse to acknowledge the artist's Jewishness, despite the well-known self-portrait whose broad brushstrokes, gesturing incompletely toward throat and chest, resemble the fringes of the tallis that might have rested there.) The painting does not take the church, that resonant symbol for Russian orthodoxy, as its focal point but rather the landscape that broods over this diminutive structure. The sky is purpled with cloud cover, the plain fertile. Bowed trees threaten to engulf the church, whose weather-beaten front huddles against the atmosphere like a laborer against the cold. A cross spindles up from its dun-colored roof. Frail, buffeted like a weathervane, the icon looks tentative. Clearly, glory is not housed within this mean structure. Instead, it resides in the munificent sweep of the sky above where clouds gather opulent, majestic, and darkly beautiful.

Chagall's provocation shares little with Levitan's coded resistance. The martyred Christ is defiantly robed in a Jewish prayer shawl in the 1938 painting *White Crucifixion* (1938) while the coral-colored church of *The Promenade* acts merely as accompaniment to Bella's pink dress and loftier spirit. And yet there is in the work of the earlier painter a resilience whose energy gestures toward Chagall's vibrant compositions. Sun plays brilliantly across snow, black rooks nest in bare March branches, and mud-splashed stalks push their way through frozen ground. Born into a land covered with ice nine months of the year, Levitan's evocation of the earth's turn toward spring seems to prefigure yearnings more openly expressed in the work of the Vitebsk-born artist who will come of age the year the celebrated landscape painter dies.

iv. History

New growth quickens in Levitan's and Chagall's canvases, but their nation's political terrain remained bleak. Early twentieth-century Russia was a place nearly impossible to feel at ease in, a country where peasants tilled the land with Stone Age tools even as the technologies of modern warfare ravaged the soil's laboriously plowed surface. The soul-churning years of violence that inaugurated the Soviet regime reached from the Baltic to the Black Seas, from Byelorussia to the Ukraine. A country of negatives, postimperial Russia was pinched and thin, with no wood to heat the frigid winter air and no bread to stop the stomach from cramping. In the five years that followed the 1917 Revolution, ten million died by violence direct or indirect: famine, war wounds, typhus contracted from filthy city water, torture practiced by the Cheka, the state's secret police.

Urban serfs without the consolation of an attachment to the land, Jewish Russians suffered well before the onset of the Revolution. In 1879, scapegoated after an attempt on the life of Tsar Alexander II, those who had managed to return to Moscow were expelled again. Retaliatory pogroms wreaked havoc through the next decade in Vitebsk, Chagall's much-loved city. After the 1905 revolution, soldiers moved into Dvinsk, home to Rothko's family. The garrison surveyed the town's Jewish residents with open hostility. By 1913, Rothko's family fled the country.

As an adult Rothko was largely apolitical. But in Russia, as an adolescent, he had flirted with the radical arguments his neighbors favored. Long years after his emigration, a residual fear shaped his translation of memory onto canvas. Stories of mass graves dug in the woods outside his hometown reappear in the rectangular depths of his mature paintings. Chagall remained in Soviet Russia until 1922, walking the same Moscow streets as Maxim Gorky and Anna Akhmatova. But in canvases like *The Burning House* (1913) and the 1940 paintings *Fire in the Snow* and *The Burning Village*, he figured spirals of smoke from pogroms in two-toned skies. To the right and left of the tallis-shrouded Jesus in *White Crucifixion* (1938), flames flicker and rise.

The point here is not simply location, location, location—though place undeniably helps define perception. At the turn of the century (as today, some would say), Russia possessed a doubled and divided sense of self. Tsarist governments displaced Jewish residents beyond the Pale because their uneasy minority status reminded the nation of its own inferiority complex. The same admixture of pride and shame that has frequently characterized Jewish identity colored this country that spans East and West but bridges neither. At the start of the twentieth century, Russia was crippled by self-doubt and derision, by too earnest a cosmopolitanism, and by a flagrant obsession with European cultural values. At the same time, Russians possessed a strong sense of their self-distinction as a people. Many of them might well have anticipated the interrogative Aciman's Uncle Vili repeats throughout *Out of Egypt*—"Are we, or aren't we?"—if without this character's unshakable satisfaction or breezy irony.

Were they, or weren't they, Russian? Paris sheltered Chagall for most of his life, but Vitebsk was home. New York lionized Rothko, and still this city was not his own. Critics who evaluate the contributions of these painters exclusively in the context of European and American ideas misunderstand their work at its core. Despite its sophistication and verve, the modernism of Paris and Berlin appeared to both Chagall and Rothko passionless and superficial, devoid of what the latter called "measure"—the sense of oppositions held in balance. The avant-garde movement of his Western contemporaries, Chagall scoffs in *My Life*, was a "revolution . . . only of the surface." Sarcastically echoing the expression that launched the French Revolution, the artist derides cubism's faddishness by defining its practitioners as self-indulgent royalists: "Let them eat their fill of their square pears on their triangular tables!" "My art," he continues, is "a wild art, a blazing quicksilver, a blue soul flashing." Sounding a note uncomfortably close to the faith he wished to distance himself from, Chagall indicts the West's "technical art" as one that made "a god of formalism." The only correct response to this apostasy, he adds dryly, is "an expiatory bath."

v. Iconographies

Madonnas, magdalens, pietàs, and a glimpse of God in a form like our own: Roman Catholicism was the half-shell that supported Western painting's birth, and cradle of its beauty. Fra Angelico's worshipful canvases offer tints pure as flowers and glossy as water. Watched over by the church officials who were his chief patrons, Michelangelo modeled the human body so precisely in frescoes that beginning physicians made these works their anatomy textbooks. It was this artist who rendered the stunning blasphemy that looks down upon us from the ceiling of the Sistine Chapel, God's human-seeming finger extended to meet Adam's yearning hand. The Vatican gave equal encouragement to Raphael, whose virtuoso compositional skills remain on view in the *Disputà* he frescoed on a library wall in the papal city. In his disputation, Raphael endowed the sacrament with dissimulating harmony and its gesticulating figures with a nobility of address. Five hundred years later, modernism remained obligated to the Church, exploiting its rebellious, intemperate palette to evoke secular magdalens. The moon flesh of Manet's *Olympia* glows starkly against the green of gardens. The Moulin Rouge dancers Toulouse Lautrec painted are gaudy daubs, their mouths streaked crimson, the mustard yellow of their evening dresses dirtied to a darker turmeric.

For centuries, the Church has provided artists both a visual rhetoric and financial support. Catholicism relies upon figures to render the supernatural in all its fleshly beauty. But the Judaism that Chagall and Rothko were born into burns away all decoration in its hunger for the word. The *word* is the world, creating light, dividing water from sky, bidding living creatures fly, creep, and walk across the land. Spoken or written, Hebrew is not means but end, its aleph and bet the calculus of a divinity people referred to only glancingly as G-d. Gaze through museum glass at the intricate beauty of an illuminated manuscript that has been defaced by time and circumstance and you know you have lost a world. But the pious can witness the fragile parchment of Dead Sea scrolls crumble into dust without complaint, knowing them to be merely the shed skin of living words.

vi. Looking Backward

Defying their families in order to paint, Chagall and Rothko produced work informed by their Jewish sensibilities. Yet their experiments with form and faith cannot be extrapolated from their sense of themselves as Russians, either. Both artists claimed their country with a rueful tenderness that never crept into the dispassionate language with which they referred to adopted homes in France and the United States. Thousands of miles away from the open space of the northern tundra and the onion domes of the Moscow skyline, decades removed from the sounds of Russian speech and the taste of pickled cabbage, this land of their birth twined itself around memory until it became synonymous with the map of their physical selves, familiar as the timbre of voice, the length of stride, the twinge in the shoulder recalling an old muscle injury. Vitebsk, Chagall figured everywhere: in the background and foreground of his canvases, in trees shimmering in the night sky, in figures dancing above church domes and housetops, in the pastel colors of flowers that reimagine perfumed scents in paint.

Home is harder to see in Rothko's abstractions. Still, an unmistakable intimacy lives in the push-me-pull-you tension of his paintings. The contours of Rothko's forms glimmer and shine. The gauzy rectangles expand and shrink. The paintings—frames without location, questions without context—feel like doorways to a deeply shadowed past. Something in their breathing presence recalls my earliest memory, home in time if not in space. At two, my small child's form stands expectantly in front of a similar black rectangle. The door is ajar (did I open it?). The gloom is infinite (will I fall off the world if I step inside?). Before the hard earth-smelling objects rain down on my head—potatoes in a cupboard, perhaps—I look out with awe and curiosity at the unbounded darkness. Gazing now at Rothko's sentient geometry, I feel equally unmoored and at home.

In the context of their country's refusal to embrace them, the nostalgia palpable in the work of Chagall and Rothko is both perplexing and touching. In memory Russia was the reedy contralto of the clarinet, or maybe borscht and sour cream, the taste of the soil in the purpled roots of beets, the tang of sky in the cloud whiteness of the curdled milk. If only in fantasy, these painters could enjoy the land's salt and sour: bread, pickles, briny herring. But how to paint a childhood idyllic only in dream? Even to choose the medium—Chagall's stained glass? the black and gray acrylics with which Rothko closed out his career?—was to displace themselves twice over, to distance themselves beyond the Pale not just of Russia but of the family's sheltering circle. Long before Rothko left Dvinsk in 1913, he had memorized the Hebraic laws that prohibit the making of iconic images. Chaim Soutine, the Belarusian artist born six years after Chagall, was badly beaten by the son of a rabbi whose portrait he had wished to paint. And Chagall? In *My Life*, the artist remembers how his father walked into the kitchen half frozen after lifting heavy barrels of herring all day. With stiffened fingers he drew from his pocket "a pile of cakes, of frozen pears" to pass out to his children with a "brown and wrinkled hand." Yet when the son he loved so dearly asked him for five rubles, the price of a month's art lessons, this man who brought "the evening . . . in with him" flung the coins in the child's face. The adult painter forgave the insult, but he never forgot "with how many tears and with what pride" he had gathered up the shiny circles.

The absence of images on the walls of Russian Jewish homes was all the more striking in a country whose meanest peasant huts gave pride of place to religious iconography. Portraits of the Madonna and Child, together with representations of the Father-Tsar, graced every Russian home. The iconography of imperial Russia's first family served as a visible reminder of the ties that had bound serf to landowner to political leader for centuries. Those of us born in the West may find the sanctification of Soviet leaders in official portraits uneasily religious, even hypocritical, but so central was hagiography to the Russian state that the portraits of Lenin and Stalin mandated for Soviet homes simply gravitated to the spaces made vacant by the Virgin and the tsar. Such was the context within which the walls of Jewish households stood resolutely bare. For Chagall as for Soutine, to make art was to insult the memory of the people who bore you, to choose the visual rhetoric of the Russian Church over your father's murmured blessing. Consulting one of Vitebsk's rabbis as a young man, Chagall confessed that the "pale face" of Christ had long troubled him. But, the painter recalls in *My Life*, he received no answers to his questions about faith. Were the Israelites "really the chosen people of God"? Would the rabbi talk to him about his work and instill in him "a little of the divine spirit"? No. Without a backward glance, Chagall "reached the door and went out."

In memory, however, he returned to his birthplace again and again. As Rothko spoke of Dvinsk, so Chagall talked of Vitebsk: in the unshadowed timbres people use when surprised into speaking what is deepest. Orlando Figes concludes *Natasha's Dance*, his cultural history of Russia, with Igor Stravinsky's strikingly romantic confession of nationalistic faith: "The smell of the Russian earth is different, and such things are impossible to forget. . . . A man has one birthplace, one fatherland, one country—he can have only one country—and the place of his birth is the most important factor in his life. . . . I did not leave Russia of my own will, even though I disliked much in my Russia and in Russia generally. Yet the right to criticize Russia is mine, because Russia is mine and because I love it, and I do not give any foreigner that right."

For Moische Segal and Marcus Rothkowitz, home was homely as the given names they buried in Russia as they fled. "Uncanny," Freud called it, this place terrifying not in its strangeness but its domesticity. The atmosphere of Vitebsk and of Dvinsk in which the artists grew to boyhood was as familiar as the opaque brightness you see behind your closed eyelids, and suffocatingly close. Living in these insular, mostly Jewish towns was like drowsing on a raft above still water, your skin warmed by sun. (It is just this quality the sentient, wavering forms of Rothko's canvases invoke.) To be home in Russia was to be safely islanded in a sea of peoples and politicians who spoke about you but never to you, thinking you inassimilable and unredeemed. Locked in a familial embrace, yearning for a different life but still loving this one: the boyhood Chagall and Rothko remembered was one you might as well call sleep.

Indeed, the crowded catalogue that closes *Call It Sleep*, Henry Roth's stunning novel of immigrant life in the New World, could equally describe the claustrophobic fellowship Chagall and Rothko knew as youths: "It was only toward sleep that every wink of the eyelids could strike a spark into the cloudy tinder of the dark, kindle out of shadowy corners of the bedroom such myriad and such vivid jets of images—of the glint on tilted beards, of the uneven shine on roller skates, of the dry light on gray stone stoops, of the tapering glitter of rails, of the oily sheen on the night-smooth rivers, of the glow on thin blonde hair, red faces, of the glow on the outstretched, open palms of legions upon legions of hands hurtling toward him." Russia was beautiful like this and also foreboding—summer light darkened by thunderheads. Somnolent but fevered, Roth's prose recalls the languorous energy of Chagall's canvases and the intimate abstractions of Rothko's work.

In the end, something deeper than politics informs their painting, just as it colors the poetry of fellow Russian Anna Akhmatova. The writer remained in St. Petersburg through the terrible years of Stalin's regime, but in "Lot's Wife" (1922–24), she expressed her painful attachment to country in terms the emigrant painters knew all too well. Choosing the vantage of exile to honor the ravaged ground under her feet, Akhmatova revisits the ruins of ancient cities to evoke the funeral pyre Russia has become. The country's wasted population is biblical in its abject misery, each death unremembered. "Who mourns one woman in a Holocaust?" Akhmatova asks, only to answer by calling the woman back to life. In this twentieth-century rewriting of Genesis, Lot's wife remains poised at the moment of departure. Shadowed by uneasiness, she hears the whisper of an imp in her ear: "It's not too late, you can look back still / At the red towers of Sodom, the place that bore you."

Despite her fear of political reprisal and her anguish at the vacancy of the country's gutted heart, Akhmatova heeded this advice. From inside her apartment she watched St. Petersburg die with excruciating slowness while she wrote of Idit's instantaneous obliteration. "Her eyes that were still turning when a bolt / Of pain shot through them, were instantly blind; / Her body turned into transparent salt, / And her swift legs were rooted to the ground." The poet's unforgiving words claw away the erotic veil that beautifies Ovid's *Metamorphoses*. The mutation Akhmatova gives us freezes the half-human form in the act of its self-destroying glance. Neck arching in a painful turn, her face inclines toward home. Back muscles cramp as her body torques toward the place that bore her.

From Israel's deserts to the cold waste of Siberia is not, after all, so long a trip: Lot's wife is transfixed, as if she were trapped under the clear ice of the Volga, her hair fanned about her face, her milky eyes cataracted by frost. Chagall's country is quick with life, but in the poet's heart, Russia remains a land of winter. "Evening Room" describes the failure of a love affair as the onset of the barren season: "Water becoming ice is slowing in / The narrow channels. / Nothing at all will happen here again, / Will ever happen." Three years later, "The Guest" possesses the same torpor. "Nothing is different," the poet writes despairingly. "Thin snow beats / Against the dining-room window-pane. / I am totally unchanged." Nothing changes—but nothing vanishes either. Like Gorky, Akhmatova was disillusioned and embittered, but she never abandoned home. In the midst of Stalin's purges, Russia was hers to mourn, and she crooned to the land in her own tongue; obliquely, yes, but full of feeling, with the shorthand of intimates.

What words could convey the awkward amalgam of feeling that rose in the hearts of Chagall and Rothko on the eve of their departure from the place that refused to claim them? Dreaming, their ears recognized Russian as their native language. Awake, they heard their Jewish names reviled in its Slavic inflections. As a nine-year-old, Rothko ate breakfast to the sounds of Yiddish and spent his school hours reciting the cheder's Talmud in fluent Hebrew. At thirty-four, as he readied himself to leave for Paris, Chagall called his life story *My Life* but lettered his canvases with Hebrew script. Stalin's regime was a nightmare for Akhmatova, Mother Russia punishing unruly behavior with a parent's sanctimonious wisdom. But Chagall and Rothko could not obtain even her angry upbraiding. To the inhabitants of the Pale, the country had nothing to say.

A wry love, a twisted smile, a strange, unhappy happiness: these were the expressions they turned toward Russia. Knowing their affection to be unrequited, they spoke of home with the proprietary, mock-despairing tenderness

Zora Neale Hurston adopted to address Black Americans in "My People! My People!" a critical but loving section of her autobiography *Dust Tracks on a Road*. Chagall wrote about his birthplace with a similar fond disparagement. The town was "boring," but "like no other"; a place he remembered, if unwillingly, "with emotion." "Enough of Vitebsk. It is finished," he announces near the close of his life story—then resurrects the city's spires and rooftops as the horizon line of his many-colored canvases. Dvinsk was darker for Rothko, a pit dug in forest earth. Nonetheless, as James Breslin notes in his biography, the artist "never felt entirely at home" in Portland or New York. The work of both painters reconciles the limbo of being born Jewish in Russia into expectancy. Indecision becomes transformative: here if nowhere else, social uncertainty and emotional ambivalence translate into tensile balance. Rothko's shimmering deracinated rectangles equivocate between surface and depth only to keep you poised upon their threshold. Wavering between earth and sky, the hovering figures of Chagall's canvases remain poised in hesitant permanency at the horizon.

Eventually, the stained glass of Moische Segal, naturalized Frenchman, bejeweled cathedrals in Europe and synagogues in the United States and Israel. Chagall crafted tapestries to adorn the Knesset and painted a dream of blue and gold and crimson on the ceiling of the Paris Opera. Marcus Rothkowitz, new American, but also "the last rabbi of western art" as Breslin notes, citing Stanley Kunitz's affectionate label, painted and repainted the large abstracts he insisted upon hanging himself, crafting a signature aesthetic that elevated painting to the "level of poignancy" he heard in the Mozart piano concertos and symphonies that played in his studio. Paint was to Rothko what song is to the cantor: the language through which the spirit speaks. His canvases are secular prayers, their radiant translucency the instrument of expression rather than its end. Rothko judged the most compelling work that which "expresses more of what one thinks than of what one sees," Breslin recounts. To look—really look—at one of the artist's works is to see through the painting to the emotional understanding that gives it shape. For all their bright sensuality, even the early canvases possess an inward austerity, a contemplative quality the comparable work of Clifford Still or Joan Miró rarely produces. The arid beauty of Rothko's later work—the series of canvases he created for Harvard University, those designed for the Four Seasons Restaurant in New

York City, and the paintings he installed at the site in Houston that would become known as the Rothko Chapel—describes a place akin to the land Genesis evokes.

Israeli American writer Naama Goldstein echoes Rothko's spatial logic in *The Place Will Comfort You*, a collection of short stories whose title could introduce any number of his canvases. "The first time I set foot there," a character Yona writes of the settlement town Margoah, north of Jerusalem, "I thought I was on the moon. I said so. But the point is, no, exactly the opposite. The point is you're exactly where you belong. . . . Sure, you're small, but you're a comma, you're a period, you're a necessary part. . . . You see exactly where you are, and what you are, what you've come from and what you're bringing about. Like Avraham in his time, the same comprehension." Rothko's paintings drive toward a similar ontology. Afterimages, residual traces, they muse upon that early union with the unseen world, Abraham's desire to hurry back "to the place where he had stood before the Lord." Rothko refused Judaism, but like the dim light of constellations we see best from the periphery of the retina, the shimmering dark of his paintings offers the clarity of his averted vision.

On the first anniversary of the October Revolution, Chagall painted the town red—literally—mobilizing artists and craftsmen until the walls of his hometown danced with his "multicolored animals." But he appropriated the iconography of the Revolution as much to express defiance toward the settled order of Vitebsk's traditional Judaism as toward the tsarist regime. The green cows and flying horses he pridefully describes in *My Life* as "swollen with Revolution" did not impress Communist leaders, who wondered what such surrealism had to do with Marx and Lenin. They were right. In truth, the artist was rebelling against the earthbound figures of Moscow's "old Jewish theatre," that Yiddish drama of "psychological naturalism and its false beards," just as he had earlier defied the old-fashioned faith of Vitebsk rabbis. Rebellious graffiti artist, Chagall splashed the unadorned walls of the town's Jewish homes with brilliant paint. "I turned the world upside down in my art like Lenin did Russia," he insists in *My Life*. Rather than work toward the Bolshevik political ideal, Chagall exploited its iconography to inaugurate a new world in his art. Ever the maverick, he turned his defiant energy upon aesthetics just as Lenin exerted his own will upon political life.

VII. Home

Even after his death he did not return
To the city that nursed him.
Going away, this man did not look back.
To him I sing this song.
Torches, night, a last embrace,
Outside in her streets the mob howling.
He sent her a curse from hell
And in heaven could not forget her.
But never, in a penitent's shirt,
Did he walk barefoot with lighted candle
Through his beloved Florence,
Perfidious, base, and irremediably home.
   —Stanley Kunitz, "Dante," from Anna Akhmatova

Strangers to the Russian Church and estranged from temple, Chagall and Rothko viewed their work through the lens of a separation sharp-edged with defiance. Rothko's father left Russia three years in advance of his wife and children but died just six months after being reunited with them in Portland, Oregon. For the rest of his life, Rothko refused to revisit the land that had precipitated this abandonment. Though he made three extensive trips through Europe, he never set foot on Russian soil again. Nor did its cityscapes and landscapes appear even in his earliest figurative canvases. He painted his mother as strong, unyielding, and melancholy. He painted his father not at all. Like the darkness that supported the shimmering bands of color in his work, Dvinsk was a force no less sorrowfully present for its willed absence.

Chagall, on the other hand, left his parents and siblings behind when he traveled to Paris in 1922 with Bella. He spent the next six decades in Europe, save for a sojourn in New York City during the Holocaust. *My Life*, the memoir he finished before leaving Moscow, is parti-colored as his canvases, by turns affectionate and sad, scornful and sure, but sustained always by longing. At its close, Chagall confesses an exile's spurned love. "Neither Imperial Russia, nor the Russia of the Soviets needs me. I am a stranger to them." Unlike Lot's wife, the artist did not hesitate before the vision of home passed from his view. But it is Akhmatova's Dante this painter most closely resembles. Insulted as a Jew in Russia, it is still Russia to whom he gives his final word: "I shall come with my wife, my child. I shall lie down near you. And, perhaps, Europe will love me and, with her, my Russia."

Going away, this man did not look back. Yet if he turned toward Europe, the proprietary caress of the closing line of *My Life* is more binding than a backward glance. Throughout the course of a long life, Chagall would travel to France and Germany, Mexico and Switzerland, Italy and Scotland. He would walk through Jerusalem, Amsterdam, Barcelona, Madrid, and New York. In 1973, a half century after his leave-taking, he would see Moscow and Leningrad once more. But the face of Vitebsk—"perfidious, base, and irremediably home"—he refused to look upon. Still, in his dream-paintings we recognize the city that nursed him, the place he could not forget, the beloved horizon of home in which he recognized not "pain," not "terror," but "strangest triumph."

LISTENING TO GERSHWIN

1. *Russia*

My favorite nursery rhyme was not about spiders or stars. Wordless, its melody still arrested my ear. As a small child I sat underneath the piano in our living room, listening—the record's faded jacket propped on my lap, the wood floor cool under my legs, the air shadowed by the curve of the instrument over my head. If music has color then this song was iridescent, a flash of spangled scales. The high notes of its piccolos rang out like the dazzle of sun on water or the trackless luster of gleaming ice.

"L'oiseau de feu," Stravinsky called his *Firebird Suite*, in the language spoken by the Russian intelligentsia before their own 1919 funeral pyre burned away all traces of the grand manner. While it played, I stared at the phoenix reproduced on the album cover. The illustration was too muted to match the music's vibrancy, but as its tones flitted in the corners of the room, the firebird seemed to hover before me. An incandescent creature, it was too brilliant to look at directly. Its wings scattered light across the wall, each feather a prism. Its heat stirred up turbulences in the surrounding air. Imagining its call rushing through Kashchei the Immortal's garden, I could almost see the flowers tousled by the waves its song created nodding gently in the great bird's wake.

Grown, I still listen to this music. When I hear it, I am transported to the suburban Boston home of my childhood: the circle of rose-colored light cast by my bedside lamp, the lisp of tree branches against the house in the windy dark, the umber piano resting in silent majesty down the hall. Then I travel beyond those sheltering walls to the gilded halls of the Paris Opera, where the 1910 première of Stravinsky's avant-garde composition turned him into a celebrity overnight. Fourteen years later, having been struck as a teenager by Stravinsky's novel rhythms, a young Brooklyn-born musician adapted their syncopations and suspensions in the first of his own classical compositions.

Hearing *Rhapsody in Blue* today, it takes many people only a first measure to recognize the rushed and jubilant pace George Gershwin announces from the start. The music's premiere performance in 1924 instantly transformed Gershwin from a Tin Pan Alley upstart into a serious composer whose drawing power superseded the Russian's own. Nonetheless, the twenty-six-year-old American was quick to claim Stravinsky as rhythmic model. In "Jazz Is the Voice of the American Soul," an essay he contributed to *Theater Magazine* in 1927, Gershwin linked the complex meter of the *Rhapsody* to the "ever accelerando" tempo of American life. Yet this indigenous music was created by a young man whose parents had left St. Petersburg only five years before his birth. No surprise that the man born as Jacob Gershovitz in New York would look to Stravinsky as mentor: the familial conversation circulating around him as a boy was conducted in an accented English punctuated by Russian phrasings and rhetorical questions shrugged off in untranslatable Yiddish. In the brash elegance of *Rhapsody in Blue* I hear the mixture of pragmatism and poetry that must have characterized that domestic speech, and as the music plays in my ears, I wonder whether in creating it Gershwin was not momentarily returned to the sound-world of St. Petersburg, city of pogrom and pleasure his parents had forsaken with eagerness and regret.

The *Firebird Suite* composed by Gershwin's foreign-born colleague claims its mixed Asian and European ancestry with more insistence. Stravinsky learned his tone color from Debussy, though France's nicer luxury could not rival his angular, edgy brilliance. Modern and Slavic, his music's chromatic tones and pentatonic structure clash with the comme il faut polish of Parisian etiquette. The Russian-trained dancers who first performed the *Firebird Suite* possessed that sprightliness of movement as common in the huts of peasants as in the tsar's opulent theater.

When I first listened to this music at the age of five, I knew nothing of Russia, the nation my father's people had fled a few years before Stravinsky composed his score in Rimksy-Korsakov's St. Petersburg dacha. But even as a young child I could hear in the *Firebird* something of this country's splendor and harshness. Now, as this music fills my Berkeley living room, the contraries of Russia's small-minded restrictions and vastness of scale are brought home to me. I see its barbarities to Jews, its exquisite Fabergé ornaments, and an entire spectrum of reds it is famous for: the maroon of sweat-stained babushkas, the rouge of chapped winter skin, the gouts of claret sprayed across the snow after Cossack lootings—and later, after my relatives began to master the sibilant sound of English fricatives, dropping "dis" and "dat" for "this" and "that"— the crimson wind-whipped flags waving high above Leningrad's newly christened square.

I am by temperament distrustful of nostalgia's extravagance, but I have only to remember Stravinsky's music to call its bittersweet pleasures to mind. Its cadences stir the dimly puzzled recognition dreams leave in their wake, intimations of thwarted attachment—as though, yearning to cross over a threshold to another life, I remain standing in the doorway. The gold of a quaking aspen burns on the tree, then glows like stained glass under the wax paper I iron in my family's Wayland kitchen. A ferry thrums quietly in the darkness of a foreign sea while my brothers and sister sleep undisturbed. A low voice speaks an untranslatable word and the brightness of red hair trembles at the edge of vision. For just a moment my brother David bends in concentration over an object I cannot make out.

What is it about music that allows the untutored alongside the professional to become receptive to such things, part memory and part want? How can waves of air create such nuanced shades of feeling? Painting offers a similar understanding, but the eye must travel from corner to center to corner before it grasps the play of color, line, and shape that composes a canvas. Reading a paragraph of prose calls for similar effort: time elapses before words can align themselves as idea in our heads. Even watching dance—an art that elides past and present as music does, each figure superimposing itself upon a prior arrangement—requires a translation of spatial designs into the language of feeling before we create meaning from movement.

Music is different. How strange to hear a piano concerto and know its beauty is simply the wake in air left by hammers striking taut strings. Still, opening the heart to the resonating atmosphere is effortless. Music speaks what is most intimate only to gesture toward ideas whose abstractness hovers beyond the limits of individual experience. This is not possession, but something nearer: the body's physiology made audible to the listening self, its ceaseless rhythms beating soft and immovable in the ear. An art of distillation, patterned sound retains a purity distinct from the clutter of words, whose freight of association dazzles and intrigues. Well played, music conforms perfectly to the beauty you hear in your head. When this concordance arrives, the rightness is so complete it transcends the blunt shape of feeling altogether.

Grown and well traveled, I hold in memory the salmon-colored limestone of Jerusalem's Wailing Wall at sunset and the glittering blue-and-gold tile of its Dome of the Rock at noon. I remember the seal-shaped glass I bought on the island of Murano resting cool and heavy in my hands and the way the vaporetti skated light as water striders over the liquid skin of the Grand Canal. I have seen gargoyles grin atop the doors of Winchester Cathedral and peered at outlandish beasts half-concealed behind the trellised borders of illuminated manuscripts in the British Museum. But nothing compares with the enchantment of that inner world I envisioned with Stravinsky's help during those long-ago afternoons.

II. America

Though George Gershwin was American born, I cannot help but imagine him stepping out of *Call It Sleep* (1934), the story of immigrant life Henry Roth set in turn-of-the-century New York. Like Roth's David Schearl, Gershwin grew up in a world that was loud, accented, cacophonous. The boats that had carried his Russian parents to the New York Harbor rose and fell on the swells like the bows of cello players drawing out the slowly vibrating low notes of their instruments, the legato motion of wrist and arm liquid as water. The chestnut polish of wood, the rounded cavernous opening smelling faintly of spruce and the ambergris of wax: the cello was perfectly framed to sound notes sonorous as ocean depths.

Arrival dashed this romantic daydream of the golden land. The squat rise of the New York coast halted the forward motion of the waves, which spluttered into dirty foam along its beaches. The Gershovitzes had left behind the elegant vistas of the Winter Palace that lent St. Petersburg its French facade, but even they, Jewish outsiders, knew the pulse of the city's Russian heartbeat sure and ceaseless as winter. New York was different, its tempo quick-stepped as a child, its mood fickle as light in a March sky.

Though a fiction, *Call It Sleep* chronicles the painful adjustment of the newcomer more profoundly than any early twentieth-century photograph or film reel managed to document. Its language permits readers to hear as well as see the faltering forward movement of the new arrivals. Rendering their broken English with pitch-perfect ear, Roth acknowledges the inevitability of assimilation without ignoring its indignities. The book opens with disembarkation only to twist salutation into a shipwreck of iron and gall. Backlit by a waning sun, a dreary Statue of Liberty looms over the boat: "To those on board who gazed, her features were charred with shadow, her depths exhausted, her masses ironed to one single plane." Expectancy has turned to grimness with the realization that "opportunity" is just a con man's pitch. Stumbling onto the New York soil, their legs accustomed to the rise and fall of the waves, the majority of Russian Jews met only what Roth called a "canceled momentum."

Like other émigrés, George and Ira Gershwin's father, Morris, wandered during the family's first years in New York. Between 1896 and 1916, as Howard Pollack notes in his comprehensive biography *George Gershwin: His Life and Work*, the family lived at more than two dozen addresses as Morris took up and discarded an equal miscellany of occupations. In the end his efforts paid off. Though he began as the archetypal itinerant peddler, he was able to provide his children a record player and a piano, privileges their neighbors did not possess. The immigrant memoirs published during Gershwin's youth offered American readers mostly Cinderella stories, but his own transformation from hyperactive street kid to Carnegie Hall impresario was more celebrated still. George quit school at fifteen, but he and his brother Ira would eventually claim possession of the city. The pianist's ragged fingernails were filed into the virtuoso's well-insured hands and the skates and hockey stick were abandoned for tails and a tux. Not long after, the family left its Brooklyn apartment for a penthouse suite on Riverside Drive George filled with three pianos and thirty European masterworks in heavily gilded frames.

Loaned in 1933 to the Art Club of Chicago, Gershwin's painting collection sported Picasso's *Absinthe Drinker*. But Pollack tells us that it included the work of distinguished Jewish painters too: Amedeo Modigliani's *Portrait of a Doctor*, Max Weber's *Religious Festival*, André Derain's *Road through the Forest*, and Marc Chagall's *Rabbi* among them. Many immigrant Jews shut the door in the face of the past, marrying Protestants and insisting their Russian childhoods had died with their Hebrew names. But Gershwin inclined his head in a gentlemanly bow toward history. Even as his parents became secular, the canvases he purchased gestured toward tradition and the sacred.

The Yiddish-speaking parents of Henry Roth's David struggle to approximate the elongated vowels of New York's place names. Rose and Morris Gershwin sounded Anglo-Saxon syllables with verve. "Ya'acov" became "Jacob" and "Jacob" turned into "George" before his father made this New World name foreign again, Pollack reports, by pronouncing it as "Judge." Once grown, however, the Gershwin children riffed on their parental inheritance with such confident, ironical élan that this accent became the city's own patronymic. The brothers' Broadway tunes were easy and elegant, the swingy, staccato rhythms unmistakably American, the blue-toned notes carrying in their modern chromaticism faint traces of temple prayers.

The nostalgic "Swanee" made the twenty-one-year-old George recognizable, but forgetfulness cemented his fame. Contemporaries listened to his music for evidence of forward motion—the faster, the better. For the most part Gershwin obliged, tuning his ears to the Brooklyn streets and their dissonant fugue of voices, an exciting urban score for the ballet of streetcars and walkers he must have watched as a child from the windows of fifth-floor walk-ups. In Hollywood, Goldwyn and Mayer transmuted this raucous life into the aerial synchronicity of film's early show tunes, directing cameramen perched high on platforms to shoot kaleidoscopic patterns of song and dance. Gershwin translated this motion into symphonic sound that created New World shine. His melodies glint like silvery cocktail dresses, their phrases shifting with casual grace from major to minor, their harmonies effortless in sound as the footwork of Fred Astaire, their voices blithe with the promise of Ira's titles: "I'll Build a Stairway to Paradise," "Fascinating Rhythm," "Strike Up the Band," "Lady Be Good," "Beginner's Luck," "'S Wonderful." Too charming for melancholy, too quizzical for artlessness, Gershwin's music asks the social butterfly and the person who favors solitude to meet in the middle. Even his quieter melodies distinguish themselves by their conspiratorial invitation to the listener, one urbane enough to craft mood rather than moodiness.

Gershwin's physicality worked in concert with his sound. From the pages of Merle Armitage's 1938 homage, *George Gershwin*, the composer's friends and colleagues insistently call attention to his vitality. Gershwin quickened the tempo at art openings, enlivened the chatter at cocktail parties, picked up the pace on golf green and tennis court. Reading these recollections, I see his lean frame thrum like New York's electrified rails—poise on its own refusing the slackness of melancholy. If he carried himself with an uprightness a shade too vigorous to be jaunty, his smile was just serene enough to suggest it was not relish but an openness to appreciation he invited.

Arrogant? Maybe, but even at twenty-six Gershwin knew he was creating musical structures to rival New York's inimitable energy. In hindsight he would provide the city a high watermark of achievement before its tempo stumbled at midcentury. And during his lifetime, by and large, the country accepted his self-confidence. Despite his dark Jewish looks and lovely charcoal eyes, Gershwin became America's golden boy, spinning off million-dollar hits with the same ease Mozart turned out minuets and trios. It was true that Gershwin assumed a polish the eighteenth-century prodigy disdained. ("My son! You are hot-tempered and impulsive in all your ways!" Mozart's father chides in a letter translated by musicologist Alfred Einstein in his 1945 study.) Still, juxtapose the portrait of Mozart you obtain from *Mozart: His Character, His Work* with the glimpses of Gershwin Armitage's book offer, and you're likely to conclude that the two composers shared a childlike delight, an irrepressible drive, and uncannily similar silhouettes.

III. Rhapsody

Gershwin aside, I can count on the fingers of one hand the composers who have made American music history. When it comes to quick recognition, even these others—Charles Ives, Duke Ellington, Virgil Thomson—must take a back seat to Gershwin and Aaron Copland, the two immigrant sons who formed our most well-known twentieth-century sound. After Gershwin's early death, Copland (a fellow New Yorker) came to greater prominence. Both musicians had grown up on streets where children tripped over the curling linoleum of cold-water flats and slammed screen doors in tempo with the sounds of scuffles outside. Copland created a quiet oasis in counterpoint to the din. In the serenity of his compositions, I also hear detachment: as a young man, he would recall in the calm, clear prose of *Music and Imagination*, he did not want art and life to "touch." Music should be "a great building that shut out the street noises."

Gershwin called this noise inside. Democratic as the downtown streets, the *Rhapsody* is breezy, affable, inviting. Scored for clarinet by Ferde Grofé, its opening slide up the scale recalls the anticipatory "A" orchestras play as they tune up onstage. When I hear its exuberant upward climb, I find myself recalling the mix of sound that rose around me as a girl from the stages where I played in youth orchestras. In memory I draw the bow of my viola across the strings while my left hand turns the pegs at its neck as I listen for the place that sounds a perfect fifth. From the solitary "A," a city of musical phrases springs up; violas calling to the other strings, winds answering brass, each instrument adding its singular notes to a world resonating with timbres too sympathetic to call dissonant.

As *Rhapsody* continues to play, the sound metropolis of the orchestra shapes itself into a different image—the tumult and tension of New York, whose crowded midtown streets open abruptly onto the wide plaza of Lincoln Center. As a teenager in 1976, I once climbed the stairs of the New York State Theater in this complex to take part in a performance of Copland's *Lincoln Portrait*. A U.S. senator introduced to us as Edward Kennedy orated its speaking part in a nasal baritone while we high schoolers suppressed giggles onstage. A half century earlier, Gershwin's own ears—barely out of adolescence—were tuned to this city celebrated for its Fifth Avenue fashions and censured in the photographs Jacob Riis took of tenements crowded as Calcutta alleys. As his colleagues looked soberly toward Europe and mimicked the prestigious romanticism of Beethoven and Brahms and Wagner, Gershwin listened for the live-wire vibrations of New York's downtown flair and uptown swank. In the twenties as now, the city hummed with the brute power of the transformer and what Henry Adams calls in "The Dynamo and the Virgin" an infinite "vertiginous" energy. This Protestant blue-blood saw in the new force only a frightening waste of spirit; leave it to the child of Russian Jews to recognize beauty in the fervent drive for innovation.

Nothing in the American classical repertoire comes close to the *Rhapsody*'s bravura. The clarinet's chromatic rush up the scale is American as a slide into home plate and Jewish as a village wedding dance, a Fifth Avenue strut with a swashbuckling nudge and wink, a street whistle that deepens into expressiveness as the music climbs upward: the melancholy brightness of klezmer stretched around the swagger of jazz. The work's boisterous slide parades its Yiddish-accented demonstrativeness, and then the piano's bass chords mime the rude life of the city, that keep-up quickstep of walkers, the jostle of feet and off-balance weaving of people hurrying along the pavement in a crowd.

Refusing a singing cantabile, Gershwin distinguishes each note. His clarity of expression lets the listener take over the bodies of different pedestrians in turn, the sounds of flute, trumpet, and piano distinct as a stiletto heel is from an oxford. As the *Rhapsody* rushes headlong toward its finish, it is almost possible to hear what Isaac Goldberg calls in *George Gershwin: A Study in American Music* a kind of "metropolitan madness." As if on cue, Gershwin stays the hurried motion, replacing the music's staccato texture in a series of stately legato phrases. Long withheld, full of yearning, their slow cadences climb upward. Hearing them, it is not difficult to imagine the thronged streets from on high. The ascending phrases seem to carry you over the Brooklyn Bridge, to circle past the New York Harbor, to dive toward coffee shops where people sit round-shouldered on top of bar stools. Soundtrack for reverie, the rising phrases speak the dreams that spiral upward with the smoke from workers' cigarettes.

Its hunger to be in and of the world advertises the *Rhapsody*'s American provenance. Indeed, Gershwin linked his composition to the life of the streets with unapologetic enthusiasm. The *Rhapsody* is "full of vulgarisms," he explained in an article for the *New York Sun* on May 7, 1930, six years after the premiere. "That's what gives it weight. I never tried to prettify it as most composers do." In the context of his sound, to be vulgar was to participate in the vigorous life of the ordinary. Ira's lyrics evoked the high life for Broadway audiences, but his brother's classical repertoire dignified the masses, the people heard pounding the pavements in the *Rhapsody*, the descendants of slaves who sang the minor-keyed gospel and blues that sustain *Porgy and Bess*. Music is the purest art, its beauty abstract as the numerical ratios that govern the intervals between notes. The Jazz Age rhythms that Gershwin's classical repertoire codified are no different, though they speak of dreams in the same breath with disappointment. Like the folk songs Copland wove a decade later into *Billy the Kid*, *Rodeo*, and *Appalachian Spring* to honor cowboys working the range as well as the Smoky Mountain poor, Gershwin's *Rhapsody in Blue* spoke with impassioned fervor for America's anonymous—its taxi drivers and railroad workers, shopgirls and sweatshop tailors.

Goldberg and Pollack both indicate that Gershwin completed the piece in his family's small West 110th Street home some three weeks after finding his name in an advertisement for the upcoming concert at the Aeolian Hall. In this piece I hear the clatter and companionship of my own house. I watch my sister, a small diva, dance in and out of the picture; I listen to my twin brothers play trumpet and trombone, their brass choir all the more vigorous for its occasional discord; I recall my mother absently call, call, call from upstairs, her voice a single violin weaving in and out of the tumult. Remembering this noisy scene I have no trouble picturing Gershwin amid his own family, writing quickly and with concentration as the sounds of pots clanging and people talking rise percussively from the floor below.

In his hurry to complete the piece he left a few piano figurations out of the score to be improvised—but that was fine, he decided, since he would be its soloist. This composure only contributed to what some called an overweening pride and what Gershwin himself labeled, in an anecdote Jerome Kern retells in Armitage's 1938 collection, "plenty of chutzpah." But eighty years and scores of illustrious performances later, his first classical concert stands out for high praise. "He didn't moon around, and he didn't get brutal," Virgil Thompson remembers of Gershwin's own performance in a November 2, 1942, review of the piece played by the NBC Symphony. Instead, he "played it straight." The twentieth-century virtuoso spoke with no less confidence in his talent than had Mozart; seeing, like that eighteenth-century artist, no reason to pretend otherwise. "I don't set myself up as a pianist, although I'll bet I can play that piece better than anybody you can name," Gershwin told the *Sun* in his 1930 interview with unassuming pride.

F. Scott Fitzgerald's Jay Gatsby touted ascots and name-dropped Oxford to camouflage his penniless beginnings. A living embodiment of Fitzgerald's "elegant young roughneck," Gershwin remained Jimmy Gatz. At twenty-two, the composer told *Edison Musical Magazine* in October 1920 that he aimed to appeal "to the great majority of our people." Fifteen years and $5 million dollars later, this goal had not changed. Others were quick to forget the Russian songs and Hebrew melodies that had sung them to sleep and swifter still to mock the greenhorns who disembarked on Ellis Island a few years after their ships had docked. Not Gershwin. In Hollywood, he hosted parties where film celebrities shared tables with refugee artists arriving in increasing numbers from Europe. He dallied with starlets and attended a concert hosted by Edward G. Robinson to hear Stravinsky play. But it was his Yiddish-speaking mother he greeted first after each of his concerts.

And if he had lived to be seventy-two, eighty-one—or even ninety, like Copland? What themes would we be humming in traffic and crooning as we coax our children toward sleep? Like Mozart's gift, Gershwin's own talent was theatrical. *The Magic Flute* offers high camp while Gershwin's 1935 *Porgy and Bess* is a salt-of-the-earth saga. Yet both composers offer range amid restriction and a lightness of touch with which to communicate depths of yearning. The elegant irony their music offers listeners appealed to innovators like Einstein,

Bellow, and Rothko, intellectuals and artists who were all too familiar at mid-century with the curbs experience sets upon expectation. In "At the Thought of Mozart," a 1956 essay published in *High Fidelity* magazine, Copland praises this prodigy for the "happy balance" he achieved "between flight and control." Copland's serene *Appalachian Spring* recalls Mozart's poise, if not his mercurial range of moods. But it is the febrile Gershwin, not his tranquil contemporary, whose music recalls the eighteenth-century composer's expressive sensibility. In *Porgy and Bess*, Gershwin checked cockiness with humility and sang of desire with an eye on the close horizon, creating a modern musical idiom simultaneously bright and bitter. Copland's tranquility offered a measured defiance of the frantic times, but I am convinced that Gershwin's temperament would never have turned moderato. He would not have relinquished the staccato rhythms of the city to take solace in the pastoral sonorities of *Billy the Kid* and *Rodeo* Copland offered listeners on the eve of World War II. Neither, I believe, would Gershwin have lost his unmitigated delight in the world—his openness to joy and sorrow that speaks to ordinary people whose limited possibilities cannot curtail the range of their interior lives.

Such is Gershwin's legacy, that it is almost impossible to imagine the rhythms of twentieth-century metropolitan life without his soundtrack. His imprint on the collective American imagination remains as permanent as Yosemite's Half Dome in an Ansel Adams photograph, as strongly etched as the face of Lincoln on the penny, as iconic as the outstretched arm of the Statue of Liberty herself. His melodies remain the jazz standards of our day: sit in a nightclub in Copenhagen or Cancún on any given evening and you are likely to hear a Gershwin number. Fusing the rhythmic hesitations he learned from Stravinsky with the syncopations of African American jazz, Gershwin created a forward-thinking music that inspired proprietary affection in the generation of Americans who claimed him as a household name. "He alone actually expresses us," Samuel Chotzinoff wrote for the *New York World* after the first performance of the 1925 *Concerto in F* at Carnegie Hall. Almost a century later Gershwin is still the present. More than eighty years after his death, "Summertime" is as familiar as "Amazing Grace"—and, as any internet search confirms, more often quoted in film and television scores than the "Star Spangled Banner." In the present moment no less than during the year it was first sung, the hard-won sweetness of "Summertime's" minor-keyed melody offers us the consummate American song of myself.

IV. Voice

A great many intellectuals responded to the misery induced by World War I by abjuring faith in feeling. Gershwin refused to echo a world-weary modernism, that dark flower inclined toward gloom. Born a twenty-year remove from the Russian Pale, he saw no need to cultivate the lassitude and cynicism other Americans pretended. He possessed no less confidence than Nobel-winning physicist Richard Feynman, Einstein's indestructible curiosity, and the tireless energy that drives the reflections of Saul Bellow's characters. "Whatever I know about music, I've wrenched out for myself," Gershwin insisted to *Life* magazine in 1929, seven years after he premiered *Rhapsody in Blue*. A modern romantic, he understood innovation as a tool in the service of communication. In his work the pain of dislocation mutates into the pleasure of translation: this, he felt in keeping with other Jewish innovators, was what art and science could offer that a more literal piety could not.

For the most part music is an art of evolution, not revolution. Its most radical innovators quote established tradition without qualm. Twelve-tone composer Arnold Schoenberg threw out tonality, then named Mozart and Bach his closest precursors. Gershwin epitomized American audacity, but his music glances back toward the Russia his parents fled a few years before his Brooklyn birth. At the heart of a spiritual like "Summertime" lies a rueful "yes" that recalls the hard lives of his grandparents. His music's spirit, a lullaby to the wealth and beauty of a culture still in its youth, bespeaks a quintessentially Old World acceptance of transience and insecurity.

I am three generations removed from my great-grandmother's passage out of Russia, but the story of her first day in New York is as clear to me as if I had disembarked alongside her. Sun glistened on the wet docks as she walked down the swaying plank that bridged ship and shore. The warm air carried the salt-smell of fish and the sweeter one of rot. On the land close by the listing ferryboat, men and women cried out words she did not know, but their wooden carts—piled high with fruit and bread and round candies wrapped in the soft pink color of her best dress—made their unknown jargon beckon. Tugging the hand that held her own, she called out for one of the pastel circles in politest Yiddish. Her mother just shook her head; the small coin her daughter asked for, the family could not afford.

A century later, my language still includes a few of this child's Yiddish phrases. As a girl, I found the drawn-out vowels and thick consonants pleasurable to pronounce and as satisfying to hear as the sounds my feet made when I walked through the field behind our house after spring rains had turned the earth to a rusty, sulfurous muck. My father denied recollection to look constantly forward, but a similar Yiddish undercurrent sustained the rise and fall of his speech. The Jewish drama, the playfulness, the half shrug that accepts the world's darkness as it mocks our position within it—all lay underneath the affectionate remonstrance he meted out on good-humored days when, wagging a finger close to my nose in mock severity, he intoned what sounded like "ich-er-de-bott-geven" (it is forbidden), the stopped gutturals and implosive consonants familiar and foreign to my ear.

Growing up in a city whose Jewish character did not preclude condescension toward greenhorns and nouveau riche alike, Gershwin and Copland must have found sound-memories like these embarrassingly close for comfort. Unlike the taunts that greeted them as boys, adult anti-Semitism was sidelong and sophisticated. Regardless of their personal distinction, each must have felt the occasional spite as a cold current in warm water. No surprise they continued to widen the distance between their music and the Russian intonations of their immigrant parents. Like Langston Hughes, Gershwin sang America, but from his childhood until his death he composed within a milieu inhabited largely by Jews. The "flashing beauty" of Maxie Rosenzweig's violin first pulled him off the streets, Isaac Goldberg recounts, and Schoenberg's tennis game kept him playing during his last year in Hollywood—or so Oscar Levant remembers in "Variations on a Gershwin Theme," his 1939 *Town and Country* tribute to the composer. In between, Gershwin attended the Yiddish musical theater that helped shape his sense of drama and traded ideas with Irving Berlin and Rubin Goldmark. Others—saxophone player Stan Getz, for one, master interpreter of Gershwin's Broadway tunes—chose to pass, marrying out of their faith and moving to more affluent localities whose covenants excluded their own families. Still, the slow vibrato of Getz's instrument recalled the reedy tenor of the cantor. Despite the shots of whiskey he slugged back to burn away memories of the Lower East Side, the Old World inflections Getz knew from boyhood and recognized in Gershwin's melodies crept back into his own musical speech.

Gershwin invited his mother, Rose, to every one of his dinner parties, where her accented English posed a good-natured satirical question mark amid the general laughter. It was this irony Gershwin scored in his music, this bemusement that forestalled smugness in his most sentimental melodies. Humor, melancholy, and playfulness were the composer's trademark inflections—all borrowed from the comedies of the Yiddish musical theater and the smiling resignation he heard in his parents' speech. A certain quizzicality, the capacity to see clearly the limitations of his own perspective, gave to Gershwin's music something that was not quite sorrow but that resonated underneath the brightness of the melodies and deepened their surface luster.

That was what immigrant parents could do for you, their rough-edged English abrading your ears till you understood the faltering gait of most peoples' hardworking lives without conscious reflection, a wisdom those born into a more settled history take years to acquire. To listen to your native tongue spoken by someone who has grown up with a different language is to be reminded that your speech offers a discrete vantage on the world. The exotic emphasis in the familiar word offers the same picture as the reverse image in the photograph: another way to see yourself. You can hear the inflections of Vitebsk and Dvinsk in Gershwin's vigorously American syntax, the way you might fleetingly register your mother's blush in your child's mobile face or your father's stubbornness in the angry set of her jaw. Like familial memory, the musical recognition is as incontrovertible as it is momentary, giving a connecting richness to the silence between notes, adding expectancy to the pitch the ear anticipates. Looking forward? Looking backward? Music is rather a state of suspension, an art in time that stops time in its tracks.

At the turn of the century, as Gershwin transformed himself from a boy who scrapped in the streets to the young man who took bows in the concert hall, the old quartet of earth, air, fire, and water was ceding to newer and less melodious-sounding players: the strong force, electromagnetism, the weak force, and gravity. Almost a century later, it is air, the invisible immensity surrounding and containing us, that remains most difficult to grasp. Music is a palliative for this incomprehensibility, the tool that quickens atmosphere into the shape of sound, the miracle by which a formless substance is made to sing. Music yokes feeling with faith and the desires of our hearts with the disregarding universe. In harmonies that resonate with feelings too subtle to name,

Gershwin found a synthesis that expressed the self while it taught him to hear the "not you" that is all the world allows. I listen to *Rhapsody in Blue*, to "The Man I Love," to "But Not for Me" and wonder which is lovelier: the resonating notes, or the quiet that returns in their wake.

v. Time

Gershwin had about two weeks—the same amount of time as did Mozart—in which to cope with the fact that he was gravely ill. At the beginning of 1937 he was tired. Some diagnosed a nervous breakdown, Hollywood's new disease. Others attributed Gershwin's abrupt loss of energy to fatigue after the completion of three films in twelve months, though he habitually worked at this crippling speed. A few intimates felt he was simply despondent at the conclusion of an unrequited infatuation for Paulette Goddard, Charlie Chaplin's companion. But in the past Gershwin had drawn knowingly upon his attachment to unattainable women, and his ebullient music was the richer for its darker undertones of feeling.

In June, excruciating headaches sent him to Los Angeles's Cedars of Lebanon Hospital, but his exam results proved inconclusive. Anxious to get back to work, he declined a spinal tap (the very procedure that, administered in his final hours, confirmed evidence of a brain tumor). After his initial release he tried to settle back into routine, but astonishingly, playing the piano had become a task rather than a given: his motor coordination was off. Within the week he had engaged a nurse and moved to the quiet home of a friend. Five days later—just weeks shy of his thirty-ninth birthday—he lapsed into a coma. By the morning of July 11 he was dead.

In the end, despite its X-rays, psychotherapy, and drug regimens, modern medicine offered Gershwin less clarity about his outcome than did the eighteenth-century physic that readied Mozart for his passing. For both composers, a mere three hundred hours spanned the interval between relatively good health and absolute cessation. Vigorous, ambitious, cheerful, and absorbed, they found their respective worlds contracting with unimaginable rapidity until length and breadth spanned only the gap between bed and nightstand. The eighteenth century was habituated to sudden acts of God and the lightning strike of misfortune: Mozart could move from the brilliant stage of *The Magic Flute* to his darkened bedroom overnight, accepting the fact that the fifteen days he possessed before rheumatic fever felled him a month short of his thirty-sixth birthday were all he would obtain.

But for the modern composer peremptorily torn away from his round of composing, piano playing, and parties, confinement in the stillness of the sickroom must have been unfathomable. Mozart spent his remaining hours dictating instructions for the *Requiem* that would become his own eulogy. Did Gershwin entertain for a moment the idea he would not live to celebrate his fortieth birthday? His astonishing joie de vivre camouflaged his body's fatigue, so it is no surprise he failed to register mortality until it hovered over his bedside. Here was a man so perpetually curious about the world a bouquet of flowers sent him rushing out for a text on horticulture; so absorbed in art he mastered painting, took up photography, amassed a library and traded dance steps with Fred Astaire; so unceasingly active he golfed, skied, fished, wrestled, boxed, lifted weights, and played tennis—all with the same competitive zeal and unswerving concentration. Irrepressibly energetic (he often punctuated his speech with a percussive beat of the left hand) and entirely joyful (he tap-danced in elevators), Gershwin was the most intensely vital individual those who crossed paths with his own would ever meet.

Friends mourned him for years, certain that behind the open door of every party they attended they would find him seated at the living room piano playing one of his own melodies. For Lillian Hellman, who left Hollywood immediately after he died, the Kodachrome city resolved instantly into black and white. A decade after his death, Vernon Duke, whose lovely "April in Paris" sounds unleavened juxtaposed to the lissome charm of Gershwin's tunes, admitted he had not accepted the idea that the composer would not write another song. Even the writer John O'Hara, who confessed to disliking Gershwin, wrote for *Newsweek* in 1940: "George died on July 11, 1937, but I don't have to believe it if I don't want to."

I get up from my desk to put a midcentury recording of Getz playing Gershwin's "Love Is Here to Stay" on my old CD player. In a former decade, the scratchy sound of the record's revolutions would have echoed the smoky timbre of the sax. Now I listen using another dying musical technology clean of sonic background as a phrase of the musician pulls against the quicker pulse of the rhythm. In the high held note that follows there is the shock of memory, and for a moment I see David again, my brother who died at thirty-one almost three decades ago, his bright orange hair vivid against the green of the armchair he is lounging in, his head cocked assertively at the angle he first affected as a shy nine-year-old. I hear his soft voice drawl out one of the interminable stories he smilingly refuses to abridge. Gershwin's brightness is my brother's sweetness. In his confirming energy I hear my refusal to mourn. Getz's luminous interpretation is a lullaby to this composer's early death, as it is an elegy for my brother's own. In the vibrato of his low notes you can detect the musician's exhalations of breath. The blurry croon of his playing tempers intensity of feeling the way a ring around the moon diffuses its bone-white beauty, the way cold air makes sharp words diffuse into soft mist around a speaker.

The shock of Gershwin's passing was only the beginning for the composer's family. Just so, divorce and distance caused alterations in my tightly bonded circle. But David's death from lung cancer created its largest devastation. For Gershwin's intimates, the emptiness of his absence must have seemed like this; a dark star, the malignant event that tore into their balanced chemistry, compounding the sharp pain of the young man's loss with the more lasting ache of familial estrangement. Surviving into their eighties, his long-lived siblings had less and less to do with one another as small spats that would have resolved at once in earlier days developed into lengthy grievances. For Ira, who functioned practically as his twin, Gershwin's death must have felt odd as an amputation, a severance more internal than external that not only divided brother from brother but the soul from itself. Ira completed the lyrics of "Love Is Here to Stay" after his brother's death. In retrospect, this song's gravely tender beauty seems to me less to honor romantic attachment than fraternal love.

VI. Memory

My gentle mother, for all her apparent pliancy, refused to enroll us in music lessons. Private instruction was expensive, but it was the ambition of Wayland's elect that rankled. Confusing diligence with aptitude, the town's elite fitted their small Mozarts with costly instruments in expectation they would bloom into prodigies. The four of us children had no such pretensions, but since the elementary school rented both strings and brass, we too were allowed to perform experiments upon its battered specimens. After school, our house vibrated with the distempered sound of an ungainly brass trio and viola, an arrhythmia that would have confused the relentless metronome of a pacemaker. But I persisted in wanting to play the piano, and at thirteen, my mother finally arranged for a teacher.

We had inherited a Steinway baby grand from my grandmother, a compact mahogany beauty whose keys my father reanimated, piano-player-like, when we coaxed him to remember a few measures of the Rachmaninoff concerto he had performed for a high school competition. Later my mother played too, her facility for sight-reading a different gift from my father's ear. When I was very young, however, the piano sat silent. To my small child's gaze it was an umber expanse glassy as the sea above the blond hardwood floor. A fine quartz crystal, my father's wedding gift to my mother, was set at an angle atop its smooth surface, its face etched with the closing couplet of Shakespeare's twenty-ninth sonnet in calligraphic script: "For thy sweet love remembered such wealth brings / That then I scorn to change my state with kings." The majesty of its sentiment would have been discordant amid the pleasant clutter of our household without the piano's elegant line and loveliness of tone. Our collie sat nearby on a worn spot in the living room rug, her head cocked quizzically to one side as occasional shrieks of rage rose from my twin brothers' room below. A green armchair, soiled with the residue of cereal spills, was positioned at the other end of the room. This was where I sat curled up most afternoons, propping a book on its frayed right arm.

The piano's polished surface gleamed in the cold New England light, exotic as a Russian grandmother at a Boston school board meeting. Which it was: the hard-won product of an immigrant daughter's dream, resettled now in the suburban home of her scientist son. From the age of thirteen until I turned eighteen, when I left Wayland, I practiced at the Steinway. We did not attend church or temple, so music was the only ritual I knew. I began with scales and arpeggios, the musical equivalent of a ballet dancer's pliés or a runner's stretches. Something in the discipline these simple exercises demanded appealed to my quick-tempered self; when I played them well, they sounded pure as the taste of cold water.

If you have been fortunate enough to attain a minimum proficiency level upon a musical instrument, you will recognize that wordless feeling of completeness that follows upon the chance execution of a piece played as perfectly as your ability allows. I practiced the Bach inventions out of a tall music book distinguished on the music stand by its pine-green front. With their fugue-like counterpoint, they were not easy to learn: one of the two independent melodies tended always to sound clearer and more rhythmic under my fingers while the other staggered, the weaker partner in a three-legged race. When I did get a piece to sound balanced, the coordination of sound was fluid as the kinetic symmetry of paired figure skaters. I liked Chopin's preludes, too, with their dreamy repeating bass lines, and a few of the Études, whose difficulty I associated with virtuoso performers and that made the fingers of my small hand ache when I played them for too long. Beethoven I loved—what teenager would not?—and I repeated the stormy opening of the *Appassionata Sonata* over and over, the fortissimo chords crashing with grandiose self-importance upon my ear. Later, when I was old enough to prefer the classicism of Mozart and Bach to the romantic composers, I practiced the second movement of Beethoven's *Moonlight Sonata*, a muted andante whose distilled loveliness requires little technique but some interpretive skill before its arpeggios transform themselves into the dynamic line of real musical expression.

My parents have long since divorced, and the piano rests silent in my brother Charles's home, my one-bedroom apartment not sufficient space to contain it. David, his twin, who stood so bashful and confident in the olive suit and bright salmon-colored tie he wore to his medical school graduation, did not live to see its displacement. The living room's grace, which I loved with a child's unconscious faith—the smooth pine floorboards against which the polished Steinway glowed—is accessible only in memory, as are the lucent words of the sonnet I had thought more permanent than the crystal upon which they had been so carefully graven. Nonetheless, I cannot help but equate their calm grandeur with the classical repertoire of the piano. Inextricably but irrevocably, I have married love to music, connecting the nuances of feeling sounded by this instrument to Shakespeare's language and the line of the piano's dark wood to the clarity of the crystal set atop its front. These days I rarely obtain the chance to play. Still, I have only to place my fingers upon piano keys and the past wells up in its resonating notes. As a child, my happiest times were those I spent islanded in the calm waters of family life that proceeded brightly all around me: the afternoons I read in the jade-colored armchair while my brothers and sister played in the kitchen, the hours I sat at the piano, the sounds of Bach and Beethoven and Schubert reverberating on its ivory keys. Now in memory I hear the chords of the *Moonlight* as they subside into silence, and the abiding family love of my childhood comes back to me.

QUESTIONS OF TRANSPORT

I

Seven hundred years ago, Dante took up a stylus and scratched the words of the *Inferno* onto parchment or wax tablet, breathing life into the Florentine language and color into the gray landscape of his exile. The long labor of writing gave shape to dreary days. Although he began the poem sometime after the city's gates shut behind him in 1302, he did not publish it until 1314, when, midway through his nineteen-year removal, he permitted copies of the manuscript to circulate through northern Italy. My edition, translated with brilliant directness by poet Robert Pinsky, has the year 1994 imprinted on its copyright page. When Dante wrote, the printing press was still more than a century away from its introduction in Europe. Any books this angry itinerant consulted as he composed his epic would have been copied by trained scribes from a noble's dusty shelf or the nascent libraries of those university towns like Bologna where he found himself sojourning.

While writing this essay in 2008, I often thought of Dante as I hoisted each week's supply of newsprint to the curb for recycling in my California hometown. A single one of these bags probably weighs more than the poet's sum of script. Sheets of vellum had to be scraped and dried and stretched before they could be inked, so parchment volumes demanded hundreds of hours of toiling. During his lifetime Dante must have handled several of these treasures, whose leather bindings would have smelled of animal hide and whose hand-cut pages were laden with pigments extracted from minerals gouged out of rock, composed from the crushed bodies of insects, or scraped from copper tools and the embers of fires and pounded powder-fine: cochineal, azurite, malachite, jet. The newsprint our eyes wander through each morning becomes the black we wash off soiled fingers. Costly as the dress of kings, the capital letters of illuminated medieval manuscripts still glitter under glass.

Like many of my contemporaries, I am fascinated by medieval art. Byzantine Madonnas offer their flat Mona Lisa smiles from the cluttered rooms of the Uffizi and the spacious halls of the Louvre. Yet whether I am visiting a foreign town or walking down familiar streets, I worship longest before showcases of old books, tracing their alphabets with devoted eyes. Worlds sprung from words, their vowels and consonants can be as large as the letters of an optometrist's chart and a thousand times more intricate. One blue capital still hovers before my inward sight, curving gracefully as Botticelli's *Birth of Venus* in sphinxlike serenity, mint-colored serifs wreathing its form in a gauzy cloud of vines.

Dedicated readers recognize that language transports them without regard to time or place. Still, it seems strange that while we can call up thousands of volumes on our computer screens within seconds, Dante lived almost bereft of books. Walking through a bookstore aisle, I stand within arm's length of perhaps a trillion letters—an unholy repetition that seems to have little to do with the careful copies made by fourteenth-century monks. But our prosaic print may also dazzle, a fact brought home to me when I worked at a Silicon Valley start-up. Hired in the early 1980s as a font digitizer amid Adobe System's then small corps of engineers, I spent most of my week alone, laboring in agreeable solitude at my desk. Here, upon a glowing screen, a procession of colossal Times New Roman letters swam with oracular grandeur. In the months that followed, I translated the shapes of this alphabet into the binary language of software with a medieval cleric's concentration, copying the slope of glyphs and capturing the weight of ascenders in a language a monastic inhabitant would have found puzzling, and with a light pen he would not have recognized. But my eyes followed the geometry of letterforms with equal pleasure.

Some thirty years later, hundreds of millions are familiar with the shapes I traced. Shrunk from their Alice-in-Wonderland height on my office monitor in Mountain View to the ordinary smallness of computer screens around the world, they continue their heedless proliferation. In the murk of throwaway sounds and scripts that besiege us, Dante's words glimmer with vivid phosphorescence. The drone of a television in the flat above my Berkeley living room gives way to the blue-jay chatter of advertisement. A car alarm blares outside my window and is silenced seconds later. A singer chants a refrain as a truck passes and its mechanical cadence ceases. But the words of the sinners hang, still, in the air. Their centuries-old voices cut clearly through the electronic noise as they shiver in frozen lakes, or run across burning stones, or shriek inside howling wildernesses of winds, their guttural accents rising from the dark to claw for my attention.

The shades thronging Hell envy the living man who walks briefly among them and prophesy spitefully in shame at being witnessed in their degradation. With their fits of pique and bitter groans, their curious questions and unrelenting anger, they vibrate with fury and fear. "Remember my memory when you return to the human world," one begs Dante. Another demands to know why a living man has come to this wasteland before his time. A third admits that infamy is more painful than dying: "'That you have caught me here amid this grief,'" he tells the poet, "'Causes me suffering worse than I endured / When I was taken from the other life.'" The Enlightenment substituted a secular chronology for Dante's religious calendar, but few eighteenth-century tracts approach the acutely modern psychological understanding that animates the fourteenth-century poet's verse. While the Dark Ages remain an icon for ignorance, the souls in the *Commedia* are our own.

II

A Jew first led me to the gates of Dante's Hell. When I was thirty years old, I surveyed the poet's "città dolente" through the eyes of Primo Levi, a man who traveled back from a different city of the dead in 1945, fifteen years before my birth. In its blasted landscape, Levi had toiled as perpetually as the shades who strain and struggle in the *Inferno*. A few years after he escaped that place, he chronicled his habituation to suffering in *Se questo è un uomo* (*If this is a man*), a book U.S. readers know as *Survival in Auschwitz*, but whose Italian title best captures its calmly incisive meditations. In this work, Levi's first venture as a writer and one that offers reflection, memoir, and travelogue alongside testimonial, the career chemist leads readers forward with the composed purpose and dispassionate voice of Dante's Virgil. Yet when Levi recalls his recitation of the twenty-sixth canto of the *Inferno* while breathing the dead air of Auschwitz, *If This Is a Man* becomes quietly exultant. I am quick to turn away from what seems the too-facile evocation of the concentration camps in film and story. But I cannot forget this prisoner's recitation of Ulysses's words as the white ash of souls disperses in Auschwitz's skies. "'So on the open sea I set forth,'" Levi declaims, no less sure of his purpose than the epic wanderer whose shade murmurs his story to Dante as "'wavering flame / Wrestles against the wind.'"

Who understands the means through which a writer crafts words that keep hold of our imaginations centuries later? If, like Odysseus, Dante ventured toward the farthest shores, we sometimes moor close to his. I recognize the thin face the Florentine writer turned away from his city as much from the portrait Stanley Kunitz offers in "Dante" (a poem he fashioned after Anna Akhmatova's verse) as from the closer likeness Boccaccio draws in his *Life of Dante*, a book he composed between 1350 and 1355 to honor his compatriot. "Even after his death he did not return / to the city that nursed him," Kunitz's translation of the Akhmatova poem begins. Before the stanza ends, I can see the recalcitrant line of Dante's bowed back and feel his heart burn for his birthplace: "He sent her a curse from hell / and in heaven could not forget her," Kunitz continues, but never did Dante "walk barefoot with lighted candle / through his beloved Florence, / perfidious, base, and irremediably home."

Each time I return to Pinsky's translation of the *Inferno*, I hear the modern poet transmute Dante's Italian into American sound. "*Nel mezzo del cammin di nostra vita, / mi ritrovai per una selva oscura*" becomes "Midway on our life's journey, I found myself / In dark woods, the right road lost." The music of "the right road lost" moves in spondees as mournful as Kunitz's "Going away this man did not look back." In the unrelenting rhythms of both poets I can follow Levi's weary, unceasing step. Asked what prompted him to translate the poem, Pinsky told a group assembled at the University of California in 1994 for a dialogue on "Image and Text," that he and artist-collaborator Michael Mazur had been "possessed by the spirit of Dante." However jestingly, Pinsky chose for his explanation a medieval frame of reference rather than the scientific vocabulary of our time—a language that possesses no synonym for "spirits" or "souls."

Initially, I found it odd that Levi would describe the ten months he spent in hell by invoking the words of a medieval Christian who had no trouble consigning all but Abraham to the same place. Odd, too, that I, part of whose family escaped the Holocaust by removing themselves from Russia and Poland forty years before war began, would want to spend so much time in the company of both writers. Equally curious was the fact that Pinsky, another Jewish American, would be fascinated by a work, as he explained at the Berkeley symposium, that consists "mostly of physical visions of the torments that Christian souls devise for themselves." Nonetheless, unlike nations, writers and readers adventure without discrimination. An Auschwitz survivor drew me instantly to Dante's intensely Christian work just as the verse of a pagan born seventy years before Christ offered Dante his own way through Hell. Levi's memoir of the Shoah may be the sole book of its kind to foreground the *Inferno*, but Pinsky is only the finest of many contemporary translators of the poem—and I, of course, am just one of many thousands of the medieval poet's twenty-first-century readers.

To yoke sin with the Holocaust, Pinsky and Mazur felt, would be to reproach the blameless, so they chose not to illustrate the Inferno's portal with Auschwitz's iron gate. But Levi did. Dante's visions shadow the modern Italian writer's memoir like the ghost that sometimes lends a televised image a fainter but constant double. If you know the first book of the *Commedia*, you will see how its images shadow the twentieth-century Italian's story. Dante's encounter with "the gray ferryman of the livid marsh" who takes his living soul across the Acheron is the palimpsest for Levi's casual mention of "our Charon" near the end of the first chapter, "The Journey." In his second chapter, "On the Bottom," Levi holds up Dante's dread at witnessing the letters "inscribed in some dark color" over the Inferno's portal in order to mirror the despair he feels waiting in Auschwitz after passing under the Arbeit Macht Frei sign (Work Makes Freedom) that translates more freely into "This Is Hell." ("One cannot think anymore," Levi writes about his numb expectancy in the anteroom of the concentration camp; "it is like being already dead.") Nowhere is the prose writer's cleaving toward Dante more visible, however, than in "The Canto of Ulysses." Levi's retelling of the epic wanderer's story forms the central chapter of *If This Is a Man*, providing postwar literature with what is arguably its most compelling demonstration of defiance.

Levi calls Dante's words to mind while dragging himself back to camp with another prisoner, the hundred-pound weight of an iron cauldron suspended upon two sagging poles between them. Because the fragments of the twenty-sixth canto restore Levi to the fellowship of those who exist far beyond the gates of what the prisoners call the *lager*, its words prove more useful than the piece of rope that holds together the chemist's ragged pants and the salvaged spoon that helps sustain him for another day.

"'Think of your breed,'" Levi recites to the prisoner walking by his side, "'for brutish ignorance / Your mettle was not made; you were made men, / To follow after knowledge and excellence.'" The soup pot sloshes its sickly gruel with each step, but the starving men think only of Homer. Audacious as Ulysses, Levi recites the story of this venturesome traveler who throws himself across barriers. Without home, family, books, or a name, 174517 weaves a net of words to cast himself and his companion beyond the humming wires and the smashing fists and the singing bullets of the lager, a "joyless kingdom of the dead" like the one Homer describes where "the senseless, burnt-out wraiths of mortals make their home." Speaking Dante's lines, Levi forgets himself and where he walks.

How startling to witness this metamorphosis: the grim horizontal that divides the soiled ground from the smoke-choked sky softening into the sea's supple surge, the stark verticals of the gray barracks blurring and swaying like green trees onshore, the empty faces around Levi become as expressive as the countenances of Ulysses's companions provoked by the words of their captain to keen, hungering attention. Dante helps Levi revisit human company: the *häftling* finds a world outside Auschwitz by replacing the "cold German phrases" that assault him there with the remembered sweetness of their Italian tongue.

Cast beyond the world of the living, Levi experiences, if only for an hour, the same eager intellection that drove the medieval poet onward in exile and the Greek hero toward the open sea. The words of all three speakers in my ear, I begin to sound the lager. Dante tells us that Ulysses and his men traveled to a similar waste at the end of the world only to weep as the prow of their vessel began to sink "beneath the surface" of the water. Shut along with Levi into the cars of a transport train that would never return them to the place where they boarded it, many of the chemist's fellow travelers must have wept as well. "One hesitates to call them living: one hesitates to call their death death," Levi later wrote about the "non-men" who struggled alongside him in the camp, the *Musselmänner* upon whose faces "not a trace of a thought can be seen." The sea has "closed up over" the Greek captain's ship. The same desolation extinguishes the last vestiges of animation in those Levi refers to simply as "the drowned." What more fitting story for the writer to recall than Ulysses's lucent despair?

Maybe what prompted Levi to dwell upon this canto of the *Inferno* was not its reflected gloom but the fierce will that casts its light against the dark landscape. Rather than urging Ulysses forward to joyful reunion, Dante consigns him to a watery grave. Still, the Christian poet lingers in Malebolge; so "yearningly," Pinsky writes, does the wandering poet's alter ego "lean" toward this celebrated shade. Dante, who took his own account from Virgil's rendering, castigates Ulysses for the arrogance of his ambition. But the medieval author must have known himself to be an equal voyager. Seven hundred years later, claiming both Homer and Dante as kin, Levi quite astonishingly describes his own journey through hell as an "adventure," explaining in an October 1986 interview with Philip Roth in the *London Review of Books* his "intense wish to understand."

The misery we know best involves the absence of suffering: the slack faces in Auschwitz that neither hear nor see; the ravaged earth of Rwanda devoid of grave markers; the warehouses in Serbia stacked with corpses whose tangled limbs are more alien than the bodies we bury. Dante makes these blank things blaze. Ulysses's resolve finds its way skyward from the bottom of Malebolge, his voice murmuring steadily within the flames of Hell.

III

To be transported to the *Inferno* is to experience a virtual reality more gripping than any created by computer graphics. Breathtaking in its cinematography, the poem encourages us to scale peaks the nineteenth-century Romantics never witnessed and to fend off imps more repulsive than any who leer from the sermons of a seventeenth-century preacher. The place burns and boils like a planet newly made. Water courses and drips through each page of its scenery: rivers of gore empty into lakes of blood, and streams of sewage trickle toward filthy ice. Part IMAX screen and part roller coaster ride, half dreamscape and half drug trip, the *Inferno* awes, fascinates, and sometimes nauseates, its word pictures bedeviling readers like black flies: the scorched skin of one whose baked features still compose a familiar face; the nails of another who snags scabs from his body as if he were scaling a fish; the teeth of a third breaking through brain as he gnaws upon the back of a head the way a starving person devours a loaf of bread.

Voyeurism may draw us into the poem, but an unconscious yearning to possess a fuller understanding of experience keeps us there—the need to shake off the half-lives we swim through daily, where bright television and computer screens distract from fear and want. Dazed by a surfeit of spectacle, we struggle to remain awake. Paradoxically, Dante's dread landscape offers an emotional vitality regular life refuses us. Some of his shades scream shrilly for attention. Others wax from muteness to moan, only to fall back into torpor. A few utter lines as rigid with despairing energy as the hand of a drowning man extended in air. If they assail, these voices also provide an intimacy we crave. In this place that gratifies no wish, the souls hunger with sharp desire: not "deadened" as T. S. Eliot writes in the 1929 essay "Dante," they are instead "in the greatest torment of which each is capable."

At the beginning of the *Inferno*, where the wind is loudest, the din jars like a clap on the ear and pounds the skull like a jackhammer battering concrete. In this place, the dead press close as trains at rush hour and shriek like steel against steel, their "strange languages" rising "in a coil / Of tumult." Hell quiets at its depths, where the pace creeps like glaciers and grinds the way wind carves rocks. The atmosphere is torpid, and as dense as Saturn's, a killing temperature zero at the bone. Dante fashions images as sharp as stalactites. Words glitter pitilessly, like fiery ice encasing bare branches. In the ninth circle, a "melancholy hole," over which "all the other rocks converge and thrust their weight," the poet looks upon "livid" spirits "locked inside the ice, / Teeth chattering the note a stork's beak makes." In Hell's still center, traitors spitted over frozen floes coldly burn, their flesh mummifying in a glassy lake as frostbite marbles their limbs. Falling tears freeze, fusing lips to silence.

And yet the measured language of the *Inferno* creates a path through the chaos it builds, guiding reader and pilgrim through sightless night. In the *Aeneid* the underworld is mist and shadow, a gray monochrome where Aeneas encounters, in Robert Fitzgerald's translation, a largely "unmemoried" throng. In this place shuttered by the simulacra of feeling, not even Dido's passionate "burning" allows "her dim form" to resolve from the dark. But Dante's words illuminate the interiors of souls as sumptuously as Caravaggio's light falls upon flesh, burnishing cheekbones and glowing in the scarlet folds of gowns. Maybe it was in the features thrown into relief by the torchlight of the poet's art that this painter found inspiration.

In the narrowing circuits of the *Inferno* Ulysses recounts his story and Ugolino grows epic in misdeed. Dante's anonymous sinners are equally famous, their miseries deeply felt despite their creator's passing. Racked and disfigured, his souls remain themselves. One spits his words in a fury, pelting the whirlwind with spite. Another musters gentle courtesy, as if he were still a figure to be reckoned with. In the canto of the suicides, a soul sighs out a wheezy breath, each word huffed out with the effort of emphysema. In the eighth circle, thieving Vanni Fucci makes the sign of the fig, gesturing obscenely toward Dante.

There is something miraculous about such strength of character. *Rich man, poor man, beggar man, thief*: in Dante's era portraiture was designed to evoke generic traits, the skills of poets as of painters planing distinct features into allegorical types. The poet's friend Giotto drafted from nature, but even this artist's radical technique gives us men and women whose expressions are more Byzantine than bourgeois.

Dante's art is different. The architecture of the *Inferno* is sublime in scale, but the faces that swim out of the dark are as homely in their suffering as the poor souls who mutter on the streets and sleep on the sidewalks of my California town. Like the living, who shift in an instant from sweetness to selfishness, the shades behave heroically one moment and gibe with petty cruelty the next. Dante left them to writhe in what is now a seven-hundred-year-old torment—without, I expect, casting a backward glance. Still, he twists a shoot in the "unmarked" woods of the suicides to hear a few broken words. Maybe in quiet moments he listened to the "wailing voices" of Florentines "grieve" again in the branches that stirred around him.

IV

On a trip to Spain in 2007 I listened to the hum of languages spoken by a living throng gathered around a celebrated painting in the Prado. Finished two hundred years after Dante published the *Commedia*, Hieronymus Bosch's *Garden of Earthly Delights* could serve as rejoinder to the poem. But while Dante remains faithful to the facts of his native city, Bosch depicts surreal landscapes strewn with oddities. Objects morph as uneasily between natural and man-made forms as do the creatures wriggling out of the pens of Pixar animators. Was that strange contraption from which people are emerging a nest of dragons, or a cave of thieves?

I could find no limbo here, nor "wood of thronging spirits," nor loving shades like those in the second circle of the *Inferno* moving "so light upon the wind." Clothed in skin, the souls in the right-most panel of Bosch's hell are filthy clogs soon to be eaten by worms. Clusters of sinners map pallid roadways through a charcoal horizon. The damned mass indiscriminately in the foreground, denied the privileges of rank they cherished in life. Were they raising their arms upward to shrink from the press of flesh? Or do they huddle together voluntarily in a futile effort to escape torment? Bodies flail and shudder below expressionless faces. Eden is just as creepy, its lawn green-minted as AstroTurf and cheerless as a retirement home. One flesh-colored skyscraper rises out of the shallows near Adam and Eve, its craggy peaks pierced by transparent cylinders that resemble the kind of Lucite rods that hold up shower curtains. The two First People stand ill at ease beside this strew of things, as if expulsion were imminent.

What moved Bosch to create this painting? Maybe, wrenched from nightmare by bells announcing the morning call to worship, he knelt at prayer before rising to Holland's hazy yellow light. *Non posse non peccare*, he might have muttered: we cannot resist sin. I looked hard at all three compositions, searching for clarity in their disordered landscapes, but skittered from scene to scene without finding ease. While lively of invention, these tableaux are soulless and unfeeling, and as replete with distractions as twenty-first-century illuminated screens.

Stymied, I stepped away from the canvas and walked out of the museum's warren of galleries into the sun. On that late spring day in Madrid the breeze moved invitingly through the cypress trees of the Retiro, the queenly park outside the Prado. Stands of rhododendrons opened up to the light, their pink and purple colors recalling the fuchsia and magenta tints of the bougainvillea on my street in Berkeley. Despite its blooming life this garden felt remote, as sequestered as the scenes Dutch artists of the Golden Age obscured behind the doors they set ajar in their painted courtyards.

Curiosity about the lives of others prompts me to travel, but when I leave home for what Elizabeth Bishop calls in "Questions of Travel," "imagined places," I remain as distant as if I were standing outside such gateways. I have seen the face Velásquez turns upon watchers from *Las Meninas*, another work that hangs inside the Prado, and have met the eye with which El Greco regards visitors from the tableau he painted in Toledo's Church of San Tomé. I have brushed shoulders with people at a Salamanca bar in the early hours of the morning and felt the press of an old woman's knees against my back at a

Madrid bullfight in the heat of afternoon. Still, I feel no closer to these living souls than to the painted self-portraits the artists worked on wood four centuries before.

A book brings other voices near my ear. In Toledo that same spring I walked a street laid out in Dante's time, past shops selling almond sweetmeats the poet might have purchased had he traveled here, and others displaying damascene bracelets the ladies to whom he dedicated his lyrics might have coveted. Where the narrow way widened into a plaza, I sat down with my copy of the *Inferno* and started to read. In the thousandth of a second it took my eyes to trace the curves of letters, the medieval poet came to me. Sallow-faced and saturnine, he recited his lines in a voice tight with exasperation. Anger pulsed in the rhythms of his cadenced lines. Eras unreeled and season chased season as my pupils traveled down stanzas. As unconscious of the mild atmosphere as of my book's rustling pages, I lingered in a city whose unreal bricks and cobbles have been trod by millions of readers before me.

V

Walk with me. This command is not one Dante urges upon readers of the *Inferno*. Instead, ever the politician, he models obliquely—through the fellowship he imagines with Virgil—the compact he desires. Still, when the classical poet instructs Dante, "Therefore I judge it best that you should choose / To follow me, and I will be your guide," the medieval writer implicitly demands we submit to his own direction. Like any author, his request is entreaty and imperative, one submitted despite his choler in a voice that mixes hope and fear. Reading and writing are twin acts of intimacy: because the bond Dante creates with Virgil is the attachment of deepest feeling in the *Inferno*, it grounds us in the poem. When the poet crosses Hell's threshold, he accepts the hand Virgil extends. At the same time, Dante reaches across oceans of time toward readers not yet born, spirits as weightless to him as the shades he walks among.

We moderns continue to acquiesce to his guidance, traveling alongside him "among things undisclosed." We earn the rapture of self-forgetting if we consent "to be drawn away," as Kafka writes in his *Diaries*, describing moments when he has fully given himself over to a book. The language that saturates the Prague writer's discussion suggests that for him as for Dante the act of reading is an act of seduction. "If one doesn't resist" the "concentrated otherness" of the writer, Kafka muses, one is "newly shaken up," only to be "brought back to one's self" with a discovery that "remains behind in one's own being."

With the help of Boccaccio I shadow Dante one morning in Siena, the city seven centuries younger than it is today. The poet has just located a book for which he has been searching in an apothecary's shop, Boccaccio writes in a passage that is as much creative nonfiction as this essay, since, he admits, he observed Dante's habit of intense study only from the "credible" reports of others. I follow the poet's lead. Maybe the leather-bound volume he asked for had been wedged in between the treatises on medicine the apothecary habitually consulted. Or perhaps the gilt lettering on its spine caught Dante's eye as he waited for a poultice to be composed. In any case, as Boccaccio indicates, once the volume was proffered, Dante leaned "against a bench in front of the apothecary's and put his book there, and began to examine it eagerly." In his cameo, Boccaccio represents Dante as a reader, and so I picture the poet this way, his thin form hunched over his prize, his unsmiling eyes studying the book-hand script with an attention bordering on concupiscence.

On the street, the tang of dust mingles with the scent of cloves. While Dante reads, young men costumed for one of the city's festival days parade by, the tremolo notes of their recorders warbling after their passing. Children scrabble among the revelers, and girls lean out of casements to watch the fencers spar below. Men in leather breeches and coarse brown cloaks jeer at the flushed faces of perspiring dandies whose silk-slashed sleeves, adorned with fur, are wet through in the heat. At dusk the files of people start to thin; women come out of doors to empty the scraps from pots; a few muse in the cooling breeze before the cries of their children draw them back inside. The sky turns red and blues to darkness. Only then does Dante look up from his book.

The poet lived much of his life alone. Or rather, he chose to confer his conversation upon those who spoke best from the pages of books. This is no doubt why, despite his overweening arrogance, his undisguised disdain for others, and his unrelenting condemnation of those who lived differently from he, my heart goes out to him. I imagine peering over his shoulder in Florence as he writes in solitude after evensong and then late into the night as the street outside his bedroom slowly empties of passersby—the framework of the *Commedia* not yet material in his mind. Downstairs, his children and the servants sleep. In the room that adjoins his own his wife too is abed, having long since ceased her cajoling. In the moonlight, water gleams from between the crevices of the cobblestone street, and I envision his window, like those of my twenty-first-century neighbors, as a yellow square lit against the darkness. Dante sits at a wooden table scored from the stroke of the ax that hewed it. Wax tablets are stacked on each side of the inkwell as if to guard the parchment from the mess of spilled wine and spattered tallow. In the shadows the small flame casts, his angular countenance grows gaunter, the dark eyes settling further under the broad brow, the prominent lines running from nose to mouth cutting deeper. The trees list and lean in the breeze outside, but the poet does not attend their swaying. Head bowed over his desk, he listens to the rasp of the stylus as the jet sheen of his words dries a duller black.

Like most writers—the bulk of us less than keen for nonstop company—I understand Dante's yearning for solitude. But such a wish was out of temper with his time. In the fourteenth century, people often slept three and four together, tore hunks from loaves of bread at meals to sop up the liquid from communal dishes of soup or stew, and rubbed the sleep from their eyes each morning while watching their faces skew in the dirty water of a shared tin bowl. Amid the crowd, the poet's "disdainful spirit," as Boccaccio writes in his *Life of Dante*, stayed "self-contained." Occupied in thought, Dante withheld reply to questions till he judged he had finished his own deliberations, rebuking the garrulousness of others with silence. I imagine him curtly civil among the babble of idle tongues that surrounded him, ready with acidulous words though regretful in privacy afterward. Intellectually fervid but emotionally aloof, he saved empathy for the characters in books.

Though quick to anger and slow to forgive, Dante labored diligently to gain the political prominence that would also further his recognition as a poet. In 1300, when he was only thirty-five, he was appointed a prior, Florence's highest honor. The following year he and two other prominent citizens were selected to meet with Pope Boniface in an effort to broker a peace between Florence's warring parties. Just before Dante reached home after the close of this papal audience, Florence suffered a coup d'état. During one of the days he spent in Siena idling in political limbo, Dante learned that his city had levied a sentence of banishment against him.

How he must have seethed to be cast so decisively beyond the arms of this city he loved. Coldly philosophical and prideful to a fault, he could neither take solace in tears nor prostrate himself at the feet of the people he despised in order to accept the terms of amnesty that would have permitted him to crawl back inside the gates. Eliot, a poet who seems to me to have possessed something of Dante's temper, pictured hell in a wrecked Europe he mourned in *The Waste Land*, shoring up the fragments of civilization—lines from the *Inferno* among them—against his ruin. Dante did not stand by the Styx and weep. Nor did he, as would Eliot, connect "nothing with nothing," listening helplessly to the broken intonations of the past. Instead, the earlier poet salvaged the Tuscan idiom if not the people who spoke it, buttressing the dazzling architecture of his poem with the polyphony of Florentine accents as he rebuilt the city stone by stone.

Most of us lob unwieldy phrases toward those who have hurt us. During the long years of his banishment, Dante sharpened the blunt instrument of language to a knife's sharp point. Faithful to the memory of others, if only in spite, he cast a baleful look homeward. From the windows of the way stations where he sat illumined by candlelight, he spat angry expressions in the faces of the men and women of Florence who had watched unmoved as the wooden gates were dragged shut behind him. "After it was the pleasure of the citizens of that fairest and most famous daughter of Rome . . . to cast me out of her dearest bosom," he wrote with withering fury in the *Convivio*, a book finished in 1308, he set to wandering. In the streets of Lucca and the mountain valleys of the Casentino he sprung phrases true as arrows to gore unrepentant hearts. From the Verona estate of Can Grande della Scala, he fashioned verses of ice to freeze souls he judged as rigid as the traitors he stationed in the ninth circle's arctic floes. By Ravenna's canals he rhymed words of censure and recrimination, his ears tuned not to the plash of water outside his door but to those whispered inflections he conjured from the place he loved and hated a hundred miles away.

Florence was "perfidious" and "base," but she remained "irremediably home." In the *Convivio*, Dante admits bitterly that he longed to end his days there. In the *Paradiso* the city walls rise redeemed in the shimmering jasper that adorns the city of God in Revelations, the material geography of Florence diffused by the poet into abstraction. But in the smoky air of the *Inferno* their silhouettes loom as if he had trained a telescope upon every crenelated feature. The poet transforms guildhalls into fortresses, resurrects the skyline denied him in the precipitous wall that rings Malebolge, and retraces its winding pathways in the stony trails he clambers up by Virgil's side. Fosse and ditch; valley and embankment; bridge, pit, beltway, and wall: every crevice and crag of the *Inferno* is composed from Florence's soil. Hell's horizon is the city's geography, the poem's atmosphere of heat and horror as thick with the anguish of the sinners as his home's piazzas were thronged with tradesmen hawking their wares on market days.

In his twenty years of exile, Dante made a wide, restless sweep through Tuscany—"wandering" as he tells us in the *Convivio*, "through almost every region to which the tongue of ours extends, a stranger, almost a beggar." He began the *Commedia* in the flower-strewn valleys of the Casentino and continued its verses while looking down upon Siena's red-tiled roofs, then polished sections of the poem by the black waters of the Adriatic and rethought stanzas as he strolled along Bologna's expansive Roman streets. In front of the pink-toned sandstone of the University of Bologna he dined amid intellectuals who warmly received him. But always the outline of Florence glimmered familiar on the page, close as the lover who rests beside you, reader, and as dear to him in the graying light of dawn.

VI

In the early morning hours my trafficked street is quiet. Outside, a few brilliant yellow squares repel the night from nearby houses. The taillights of a passing car slide red and silent across the window casing before they vanish. I imagine looking down upon this place from a plane, watching the city glimmering remote below the glass, its illumination colder than starlight and seemingly no closer. Is it contact I crave from Dante's world, a closeness his language invites? Am I simply bedazzled by the medieval world of my imagining, a place of purer color than our own, if of equally transfixing cruelty? Or is my cleaving to this Christian some deeper yearning, a wonder about what it would be to exist as someone else?

In Dante's time Christianity was compulsory throughout Europe, its rituals the calendar by which life took measure. "Progress through the liturgical order was the closest thing to an agreed-upon time scheme for the London day," Paul Strohm writes of that city in *Chaucer's Tale: 1386 and the Road to Canterbury*. Florentines also parsed their time according to the sacred calendar. They were married according to the Church's rules, castigated by its law, physicked by its medicine, and taught by its books. The rigid rhythms of Christian prayers settled their nerves against the innumerable hazards that could yank them from the arms of the world without a whisper of warning. And yet, for all the Church's sureties, its life insurance could not stay the terrors that crept nightly to their thresholds to wait like massy shadows in the moonlight outside.

In the Middle Ages the afterlife was not a mirage glimmering far away on the temporal horizon. It was a side street a man or woman turned down absentmindedly when some everyday disaster caused him to lose his way—a cut turned septic, a misstep from a tower window, a fever brought on by typhus or the plague. Unshriven, unrepentant, or just unfortunate—the victim of a landslide or a spring storm—the resident woke to the stink of scalded flesh and the jeers of demons crowding him cliffside. Hell received impartially, welcoming the wicked alongside the unwary. The first and fullest democracy, its gate lay open, a threshold no one was denied.

"ABANDON ALL HOPE, YOU WHO ENTER HERE": the phrase "inscribed in some dark color" over the portal of the Inferno remains the poem's most famous line. How strange that Hell's most dreadful vision is a sentence, not a sight. The computer-printed capitals glare from the page of my paperback copy of the *Inferno*, their black magnificence no less scourging there, or on the page of this book, than in the hour Dante first impressed them onto parchment. "Help me escape this evil that I face," he pleads of Virgil at the outset of the *Inferno*. As I read, I see Dante hesitate as he stands under this stone inscription. Then together we turn again to the Roman at Dante's side. I study these pitiless letters and know why the medieval poet asks another to "make clear / Their meaning, which I find too hard to gather." But why appeal to *Virgil* for aid rather than to a fellow Catholic author? How can a pagan lead Dante to "Saint Peter's gate," interceding with "the God" the Roman "did not know"?

For an answer I return to Primo Levi, my own first guide to the *Inferno*, a man led through a modern "città dolente" by a writer who did not share his faith. In Auschwitz Levi recited Dante, refusing to resist the "concentrated otherness" of this Christian whose book praises the God in whose name Levi and countless other Jews had been condemned to hell. To my mind there is no more generous gesture for one who suffered in the Holocaust than to "be made into his counterpart," as Kafka writes in the *Diaries* of the relationship between reader and writer. But of course, Levi, letting himself be drawn away by Dante, returns to himself, the excursion of reading affording the modern writer renewed understanding, as he indicates in *Se cuesto è un uomo*.

If words can destroy hope, they can also rebuild trust. Levi survived the long months in a concentration camp by believing in a writer across the gulf of faith. Dante, too, must have been sustained in exile less by his reverence for religion than by his faith in books. Reading seems the purest act of grace, a forgiveness that transforms condemnation into curiosity and enables us to bridge the deepest chasms of thought and belief. Both Dante and Levi, absorbed readers, refused in their turn the isolating path. By consenting to let the words of other writers speak their minds, they found a way to resist the separation of souls in this world—and perhaps, the faithful might say, the loneliness of those divided in the next.

VII

Like open-heart surgery and prayer, writing and reading are not always efficacious. Levi freed himself from Auschwitz with Dante's help, but the death camps made transport brutish, a conveyance that battered the body and did not sustain the soul. The chemist returned to Turin after the war and settled in to work at a paint factory outside the city, but—Carole Angier tells us in her biography *The Double Bond*—the writer did not return home. Instead, he hovered on the outskirts of his birthplace, spending his weeknights in the company's dormitory, where he finished a draft of *Se questo è un uomo*. In the ensuing years, he worked full-time as a scientist but continued to publish steadily, authoring several semi-autobiographical works, a novel, a second book about Auschwitz (*The Drowned and the Saved*), and a wealth of stories—many of which returned him to wartime terrors.

Seventeen fictions that appeared posthumously in English in 2007 under the title *A Tranquil Star* reveal how Levi's hellish history remained closely present for him. In some stories, such as "The Death of Marinese," we travel alongside Levi directly back to the battlefield. Others gesture toward World War II by musing about the ethical questions that conflict engendered. Both "The Knall," an ostensibly lighthearted exploration of a toy that kills, and "Gladiators," which relocates the appetite for voyeurism in an unspecified future, chart, as Ann Goldstein notes in the collection's introduction, what Levi called in a letter to his publisher—"an unraveling in the world ... that annihilates one or another aspect of ... our moral universe." Read with the advantage of hindsight, "Bureau of Statistics"—reminiscent of Kafka and Borges—augurs

Levi's suicidal fall from his apartment building in 1987. The story describes a fifty-eight-year-old character as one who "doesn't fear death and doesn't seek it, either," but who "may act carelessly." Assigned not only to explain the death but to invent its cause, Arrigo, the writer's proxy, has "him fall from a scaffold: he wouldn't suffer much."

Varied in tone, these stories share a quality of loneliness. Barely perceptible, this isolation is the more remarkable for its gentleness of expression: as though Levi could not bear to stay too long in human form, he moves fitfully from shape to shape through the mostly third-person narrations of his book.

In "Buffet Dinner," a parable about the estrangement survivors experience after reentering what the *Inferno* labels "the human world," the narrator slips inside a kangaroo that must negotiate a party despite his obvious difference, privy to casual commentary about his species' near extermination and the indifference of others to his perception of this trauma. In "The T.V. Fans from Delta Cep." the central character is transported to the depths of space. This personage, an alien who writes to the host of a popular television show from light years away, is chatty and charming; however, even though the words of his letter are clear, his signature remains "illegible."

But even this far-flung voice is more down-to-earth than the narrator of "In the Park." At the outset of this story, Antonio is welcomed to the shores of the afterworld—not the place humans go but a more exotic composite where characters from books find housing. Antonio is as closely linked to the author of the autobiography Levi invents in this story as the narrator of *Se questo è un uomo* is to the writer himself—yet the chemist does not hesitate to obliterate the memory of this fictive personage. As Antonio grows diaphanous in the final paragraph, he understands his time is near. "His testimony complete," he sits under a tree waiting "for his flesh and his spirit to dissolve into light and wind."

As an allegory of Levi's postwar experience, "In the Park" is no less transparent than its fading hero. Its landscape parodies the *Inferno*, affording readers a self-consciously breezy tour of literature's afterlife that provides the writer momentary escape from the survivor's lingering sorrow even as he testifies to its lasting estrangement. Here as elsewhere in *A Tranquil Star*, transformation is forgetfulness, an effort to take flight from the human as much as to reaffirm social ties. Circe changes men into pigs in *The Odyssey*, but the sailors' swinish language is just trickery, a metaphor Homer exploits to condemn our unchanging gluttony for acquisition. Levi's late stories are closer in spirit to the metamorphoses of Ovid and Kafka because here, also, men and women do not return to themselves. The modern writer's stories originate from a secular sensibility preoccupied with chance rather than the ordered world of Dante's faith, but they illuminate the extent to which Levi, too, remained exiled.

VIII

What reader has not sometime hoped for the shock of transcendence, the bolt of lightning that seizes? I search for words brilliant enough to weld "now" to "then" and grope for a language that will bind my imagination to the writer's understanding, making us twin witnesses to one scene. In Levi and Dante I find this transport, though it is no kin to rapture. In their pages I meet spirits so bereft they could have been torn away from the warm tissue of the lungs and the heart's comforting murmur. Harder to witness but more deliberate, their twin conveyance of souls is neither a delusional effort to slip the skin nor the romance of easy union with another.

"I spoke / Like one set free," Dante tells us in the *Inferno*'s second canto, after Virgil's narration has restored his "spirit. Now, on," the medieval wanderer insists: "For I feel eager / To go with you, and cleave to my first intention / From now, we two will share one will together." Writing wrenches but also permits reunion. Reading likewise cleaves the self twice over, duplicating as it divides: when we lose ourselves in a book, we acquire the "senses, affections, and passions" Shylock demands we look for in those we malign. From a writer's words we may obtain the "quality of mercy" Portia pleads for listeners to find. The voyage of reading is often dismissed as a flight from reality, but is life less escapist than art? What is experience, after all, but a set of shadows that chase themselves across the skull's bone? Just as the hand that holds the book is out of focus, and the place where we read a blur beyond the page, the souls of others hover indistinctly on the horizon of consciousness. Absorbed in the closed worlds of our thoughts and feelings—wild woods of neurons as savage as Dante's *selva oscura*—we can turn to language that demands we see others more clearly, or we can settle for a televised babble that does little more than beguile.

Contemporary citizens possess no greater insight into injustice than did Dante when he mourned the finest souls confined in limbo. We can offer no better explanation for cruelty than could Primo Levi, who witnessed the blameless scourged in hell. My younger self nodded approbation when hearing philosophers and critics untwist the skeins of ethics from the woof of aesthetics. Older now, preferring to look for parallels rather than to divine distinctions, I trace the upward arc of the "e" these two words share, follow the symmetry of their common "c," track the grace-note serif that completes the "t," and admire the swan's-neck curves of each lovely "s." Then, as has no doubt been the case for other readers who have picked up the *Inferno* and yearned for a glance at the outermost shores, I find that the clarity of letters blurs into the dark marks of its words. I listen while the flame of Ulysses speaks from the mind of a man who wrote in rooms long since fallen to dust, the layers of other lives in medieval Bologna and Ravenna and Siena pressed close by time, the rutted street still outside worn smooth by a seeming infinitude of walkers.

The flimsy spine of my paperback *Inferno* gathers the centuries as closely as the stitches of Dante's fourteenth-century manuscript once bound its vellum pages. I read outside my flat and the days spool past like those years in a blur of sound half-heard and image half-noticed. A breeze fans my skin, recalling me to the body from which I have slipped away. I look up from a paragraph and watch the moving leaves transmute the invisible world, for a moment, into something seen. In the words writers craft as finely as clerics once labored over illuminated letters, I find an equal intimation of presence, a perception if not a place, an indifferent divinity conferred in an ordinary moment of grace. As I sit with a book and the traffic falls to a hush, the wind stirs a chime to music not unlike the voices Dante might have heard. Then there comes to me a trace of the awe the faithful must know when they are visited by that great beating of wings: a faint, ardent sublime.

IN PRAISE OF BELLOW

Looking for grace under pressure? Don't pick up Saul Bellow. You crack one of the novelist's fictions only to be accosted by a stranger in manic contemplation of experience. Modernism's stream of consciousness gives us preternatural hearing to capture unspoken musings. But with Bellow there is no need to strain our ears. His characters clamor for consideration. Their interior monologues are not desultory fragment but purposeful argument, their urgent voices closer kin to the dramas of Arthur Miller and David Mamet than to the novels of Woolf, Joyce, and Faulkner. Of varying vocations, these characters all wish to sell us on the soul. Impatient and impassioned and on the verge of panic at the shortness of life, they demand we give them all our time. Through their meditations—one-sided conversations—they communicate to us their desire for presence and their sensuous metaphysics. Overheated and undignified, often thrice-married and mostly over fifty, they are cognizant that the world remains indifferent to human improvement. Still they stumble forward, overtired and joyful. Think. Love. Act, they tell us, like a chorus of modern-day Marvells coaxing readers away from coyness. Better devour your time, they urge, than waste a second with consciousness set on idle.

Such energetic cheerfulness flies in the face of Jewish American literary custom. Since the late sixties, bookstore shelves have groaned under the weight of Holocaust publishing. These days, writers announce their virtuosity by grappling with this central negation early in their careers: Nathan Englander's first story collection included "Tumblers" (the Shoah as told by the Fools of Chelm), Lara Vapnyar's debut opened with "There Are Jews in My House" (the Shoah as witnessed from inside Russia), Nicole Krauss cracked the bestseller list with *The History of Love* (the Shoah as narrated through a kvetch), and

Jonathan Safran Foer garnered a movie deal with his first novel *Everything Is Illuminated* (the Shoah as foretold from the shtetl). But the well-established also persistently sound this subject. Novelist Michael Chabon won a Pulitzer with *The Amazing Adventures of Kavalier and Clay*, as did artist-writer Art Spiegelman for *Maus*. Francine Prose's *A Changed Man* featured a Holocaust survivor, and Philip Roth time-traveled back to the 1940s in *The Plot against America*. In 2005, sixty years after the close of World War II, Cynthia Ozick named "the effect of the mass murder of one-third of the world's Jewish population" our most "profoundly Jewish theme."

Throughout his distinguished career, Bellow merely swatted away talk of authorial obligation. Had he lived long enough to read Ozick's doleful essay, "Tradition and the Jewish Writer," he would have wasted no time lancing its bombast. Sententiousness set his teeth on edge ("Major statements are hot air," Charlie Citrine scolds in *Humboldt's Gift*), while the crawling pace of grave pronouncements irritated his mercurial intelligence. In *Herzog*, Bellow chides gloom as self-indulgence, reproaching lugubriousness in his tartest voice. Our collective sense of "grievance" has become a "murdering imagination," Moses reflects in this novel's pages. "Well, there is a piece of famous advice, grand advice even if it is German, to forget what you can't bear." Like Grace Paley's flippancy in "The Immigrant Story" ("Rosiness is not a worse windowpane than gloomy gray when viewing the world," a character remarks there), Bellow's offhandedness was a study in noncompliance. He simply had no truck with language that touted disaster writ large. Suffering he understood—as what feeling person does not?—but despair was intellectual sloth. "Nothing 'normal' holds the slightest interest," he complained in a 1991 interview with Boston University's literary magazine *Bostonia*. "Spare us the maiden joys of Tolstoy's Natasha. . . . The top ratings are permanently assigned to Auschwitz, Treblinka, and the Gulag."

Rather than eulogize the victims of the death camps, Bellow celebrated the lives of their American relatives through unrepentantly exuberant characters such as Herzog, Humboldt, and Ravelstein. Augie March, whose picaresque adventures rival the freewheeling exploits of Henry Fielding's *Tom Jones*, inaugurated this approach in 1953. "Evidence of a decision not to surrender to horror," as Bellow mused in Philip Roth's 2000 essay for the *New Yorker*, Augie does not so much deny history as tell it slant, fictionalizing the Bellow family's immigrant experience rather than chronicling the story of their extended family who never left Russia.

Even *Mr. Sammler's Planet*, the author's own Holocaust book, is markedly short on trauma. Polish-born Artur Sammler has no use for mourning. Indicting the foolishness of Americans who insist upon venerating him as a "symbolic character," Sammler is more concerned with the state of late twentieth-century America than with Europe's catastrophe. Indicted by critics as callous upon its publication in 1970, the novel still managed to garner Bellow a third National Book Award (because, one wonders, it invoked the Shoah, however glancingly?). Yet *Mr. Sammler's Planet* represents the Holocaust only to contextualize its devastation. "I don't know whether humankind is really all that much worse," the ex–Auschwitz inmate reflects toward the book's close. "In one day, Caesar massacred the Tencteri, four hundred and thirty thousand souls." Like Hitler, his twentieth-century successor, the Roman dictator launched his politically self-aggrandizing attack during an armistice, Sammler explains. For Bellow, modern trauma merely reiterates ancient genocide. To readers who expected this disaster to be rendered as singular "stain" upon our "moral nature," he had little to say.

In a 1965 interview for *Glamour*—Herzog's many months on the bestseller list had made him a household name—Bellow shepherded Gloria Steinem around Chicago. Under his eye and her pen the place looked urban and upbeat, hard-edged but soft-hearted. Along Maxwell Street, "a district full of . . . cheap merchandise," she recalled, Bellow bantered with Yiddish-speaking shop owners. A salesman lingering in a doorway exchanged a few words and shook the novelist's hand. Bellow translated for Steinem: "I asked him if he was praying." The shopkeeper wasted no time returning his rejoinder with Old World aplomb: "God is an old man who sleeps all day. Why should I disturb him?" Farther down the street, the writer exchanged Talmudic quotations with a pushcart peddler. Turning away from his display of plastic jewelry, the peddler offered this parting shot: "Death awaits us all."

The same wry humor sustains Bellow's characters, who understand death as prosaic fact rather than the occasion for operatic wailing. Philip Roth praises *Herzog* as a "richer novel" than *Augie March* and *Henderson the Rain King* because it offers "a brand of suffering . . . largely precluded" from the later novels. But just listen to Moses's admission at the opening of *Herzog*: "I hate the victim bit." And after retreating to his house in the Berkshires: "Grief, Sir, is a species of idleness." Later still, "suffering is another bad habit. . . . We must improve." And finally: "I am willing without further exercise in pain to open my heart."

In line with conventionally lachrymose accounts of Jewish history, Roth abbreviates experience as affliction. But Bellow's characters rarely speak in the melancholy accent many Jews and non-Jews alike take to be characteristic of Jewish sensibility. For the chronic Murphy's Law sigh of acquiescence, we need to go to a novel like Nicole Krauss's *History of Love*. In this book, octogenarian survivor Leo Gursky sings the blue-toned notes Zero Mostel's Tevye made famous on Broadway, cadences that have provided Americans with their cheerfully mournful key signature for Jewish living since the debut of *Fiddler on the Roof*. Krauss provides deft illustration of drag-yourself-forward-another-step-though-it-means-scuttling-crabwise-on-your-hands-and-knees Jewish stubbornness. Poster boy for osteoporosis, Gursky splutters into high gear when provoked. Larger than life, someone says; and, like an old battery with a charge alive at its corroded core, he jumpstarts himself forward: "What is larger than life?"

Gursky is delightful, but were he in a Bellow drama he would never occupy a central role. His body slumped expressively in a Yiddish shrug of the shoulder before the inevitable gall and wormwood, Gursky sports little of Herzog's energy or Ravelstein's extravagantly sensual aesthetic. Even in *Seize the Day*, a book Bellow would come to reject for its "victim" mentality, the writer refuses to drag his characters to the "wat'ry" depths of Lycidas he quotes within its pages. From first page to last word, his people are all inquiring spirits whose panoply of humiliations never dims the expectant gaze they turn upon experience. Conceived fifty years apart, Augie and Ravelstein share a knockabout roughness. Despite their calluses, they are enamored with the mystery of their own existence. Open either novel and watch language gush like water from a hydrant. These characters hum with energy, they blaze with unsuppressed curiosity, they radiate hope the way suns make hydrogen. Moderns, they do not refuse marvel but remain as oblivious to the age's boredom as if they had been born into the sixteenth century.

This is Bellow's gift, to offer you the ridiculously open hearts of men over fifty who begin each day with the high expectations a ten-year-old brings to a birthday party. Cheerful crazies whom the more self-contained edge away from and the decorous view askance, his characters are always characters. But watching them run spastically forward toward their windmills, you cannot help but trail after them with an involvement akin to faith. Backhanded by a century whose ill will swells to pandemic proportions, they refuse hardness. In the face of the spiritless, they speak without embarrassment of the soul.

The novelists who published in the generation before Bellow were in their own ways hard on "society," but they delivered their censure more composedly. Jay Gatsby, Jake Barnes, even J. Alfred Prufrock—such elegiac figures carry themselves with stoicism and dignity. By contrast, the charm of Bellow's central characters lies in their ungainly vitality. Even *Seize the Day*'s Tommy looks out at the world without demanding from it the deceiving loveliness of lyricism. Here no mermaids comb the white hair of the waves blown back while singing each to each. In their place we are offered the brackish beauty of Lake Michigan, whose dank mop water smell mixes pleasingly with the sounds of "pianos, and the voices of men and women singing scales and opera, all mixed, and the sounds of pigeons on the ledges." Awkward, foolish, and vibrant: this is experience, for Bellow. The sirens don't sing to you, but pigeons will, their small heads cocked as they look for crumbs left by passersby on the pavement below.

Seize the Day eventually makes good on its carpe diem claim, if only to chart the collapse of its central character in a sumptuous display of grief. Bellow's tongue is caustic and his eye merciless. Yet the lavishness with which Tommy mourns his failures testifies to the novelist's buoyant energy. There is something transforming in the spectacle of such graceless sobbing, a triumphant embrace of feeling that refuses to be shushed into stillness. In a novel whose lyric correctness begins by internalizing as it scorns the well-bred austerity of 1920s modernism, the "great and happy oblivion" of its tear-blinded close refuses to be shamed into quietude. Within its pages, as more tellingly in *Augie*, *Herzog*, and *Ravelstein*, Bellow delights in Jewish volubility despite (or to spite) its dissonance with the self-contained severity of Puritan prose tradition. *Seize the Day* is his sardonic alternative to Miltonic and Eliotian elegy, an open-throated release whose sloppiness cheerfully rebukes the elegant withholding of their guarded hearts.

The American minds we inhabit in Bellow's novels reject the poise we find elsewhere in midwestern and East Coast writers and everywhere in Fitzgerald, Hemingway, Frost, and Eliot. In style and substance the moderns are spare, crystalline, and beautiful, throwing out costly phrases such as Nick's offhand description of Gatsby—"he dispensed starlight to casual moths"—as if these gems demanded no effort. Taking sprezzatura as their characteristic mode, the expatriates of the twenties and thirties affected lightness even as the twentieth-century sky turned dark. They favored the steely control of ballet, that lissome art of transforming hard work into liquid moves.

Jewish to the core, Bellow's postwar characters seem bent on making what is simple look vastly complicated. They are all wasted energy and effervescent motion, their mobile faces expressive of a Shakespearean range of feeling, their fevered gestures bewildering listeners who try to follow their labile trains of thought. They stumble, fumble, and flail. They wave their arms, trip over furniture, and hyperventilate. They announce themselves rather than waiting to be introduced. And so we are treated to Augie March's famous opening lines in the novel Bellow proudly and retrospectively called his first "incorrect" book: "I am an American, Chicago born—Chicago, that somber city—and go at things as I have taught myself, free-style, and will make the record in my own way." Handsome and high-colored, peripatetic and itinerant, convinced they are destined for greatness but forever mistiming their approaches, such characters possess neither sangfroid nor serenity. Still, they have the wit to satirize their own shortcomings.

Bernard Malamud's protagonists are equally concerned with ethical questions and Philip Roth's narrators are often as clever. But in the post–World War II years, only Bellow's people possessed a breezy shamelessness that appealed simultaneously to the children of immigrants and the daughters and sons of the native born. Throwing off the angst their Russian-born parents carried in the set of their bones, Bellow's characters refused to take on the Puritan howling-wilderness inferiority complex, with its guilt over witch burnings and its ever-present sexual anxieties. Unabashed, they transformed the minor-keyed inflections of their Yiddish-speaking parents into a joyful secular idiom Americans heard as their own.

In the bombed-out bleakness of the post–World War II Paris streets, the winter damp possessed none of the beauty Hemingway knew in the 1920s and captured in *A Moveable Feast*. His city enraptured even in December. It was a place where the sighs of expiring poets breathed life into writers like him whose ears were keen to hear them. "All of the sadness of the city came suddenly with the first cold rains of winter," Hemingway remembered, "and there were no more tops to the high white houses as you walked but only the wet blackness of the street and the closed doors of the small shops, the herb sellers, the stationery and the newspaper shops, the midwife—second class—and the hotel where Verlaine had died where I had a room on the top floor where I worked." In 1948, when Bellow arrived, the chill was Dickensian. The Paris "gloom," he recalled to Philip Roth in a series of remarks the *New Yorker* published two weeks after Bellow's death, lay everywhere "heavy and vile." Even the Seine was unlovely, smelling "like some medical mixture." In the wake of Vichy, there was no more poetry, only a self-contempt too enervated to muster spite. The concession of weakness had made the French descend from the high horse of the cavalier to the creeping life of cynicism. Collaboration showed in the guilty cast of the postwar faces, which, turned toward their American liberators, reflected only derision. Bellow had a Jewish explanation for this: "bad conscience." Only too happy to pop the balloon of French glamour ("they pretended that there was a vast underground throughout the war, but the fact seemed to be that they had spent the war years scrounging for food in the countryside"), he refused to reinvigorate the modernist fable of the Jazz Age.

The visitor from Chicago was a greenhorn in this "sullen, grumbling, drizzling city," he indicated to Monroe Engel, his editor at Viking. Paris was determined to depress him—no one could claim he lacked ego—and the novelist obliged for a while. "I seem," he recalled dryly in Roth's *New Yorker* essay, "to have been a good solid sufferer in my youth." *And yet*, as Nicole Krauss's appealing octogenarian Leo Gursky would say. The Americans had liberated the city; now, insisted the arriviste, "it was time for Paris to do something for me." Halfway through the dismal hospital novel he was writing, Bellow underwent a change of heart. As he watched the street sweepers sluice the grimy roads, the water's "sunny iridescence" transformed the gutter into a vision of beauty. "Just the sort of thing," he remembered a half century later for Roth, "that makes us loonies cheerful."

In *The Adventures of Augie March*, he translated this epiphany into an original American sentence that was philosophic and pragmatic—a "fusion," he explained, "of colloquialism and elegance." The ruins still smoldered. The reproachful eyes of six million ghosts were fixed on Europe. And Saul Bellow confirmed—what else?—that being Jewish was a gift. The supercilious faces around him quickly shuttered themselves in the presence of Yiddish-speaking immigrants. Well then, he would write about these people whose verbal swagger did not successfully camouflage their efforts to appear habituated. Though they were American-born, his characters had been schooled in the quizzical accents of Russian, Polish, and Hungarian parents. "Everybody wished to be an American," the author commented of the postwar generation in a 1984 interview with *TriQuarterly*. Their open "secret" was that they "hadn't succeeded in becoming one." Instead of apologizing for the emotional extravagance that kept them on the periphery, Bellow made their high color a central fact of American life.

No more gracefully subdued Winslow Homer watercolors or Sargent portraits in oil, their brushwork too fine to be examined. As Pollock's wildly energetic drip paintings came to represent the postwar period, Bellow's intemperate prose was claimed by the age. The only novelist to garner three National Book Awards, he also picked up the Pulitzer, the National Book Award Foundation Medal, and the Nobel along the way. In 1964 *Herzog* became a bestseller, and Bellow rich at last. Herzog (a Moses, after all), made American readers see the world through Jewish eyes—not the guttered stare of the death camps but the alert gaze of the sons and daughters whose lucky parents had escaped unscathed.

A liability becomes an asset, the ticket with which you hold the world at attention. Bellow perceived his Jewishness both as prosaic fact and marvelously unearned reward, the "piece of good fortune," he told the *Chicago Review* in 1972, "with which one doesn't quarrel." In his novels, a tremulous joy in the beauty of this world—the same lightheartedness you see in Chagall's shimmering canvases—also communicates reverence for the next. Herzog is "out of his mind" but "all right," scribbling feverishly amid the scaling paint and rat droppings of his vacant house in the Berkshires with "a corner of his mind . . . open to the external world." The body stays earthbound, sharing bread with the mice, sleeping on a grimy mattress without benefit of sheets, but the mind aspires for the violet beauty of the air. Opening his eyes in the dark, Herzog recognizes that "the stars were near like spiritual bodies. Fires, of course; gases—minerals, heat, atoms, but eloquent at five in the morning to a man lying in a hammock wrapped in his overcoat." In this novel there is no chest-constricting swallowing of derision but rather expansion, a rush of feeling too strong to be thwarted. To be unmoored is not punishment but possibility.

The consciousness of a sixty-year-old is not a sales pitch most literary agents would salivate over, but Bellow holds readers accountable to his aging characters. Even more than their plotlessness ("a guy wanders around," Scott Turow deadpanned in "Missing Bellow"), his books are distinguished by an effort to meet "the stubborn fact of death." "Ignorance of death is destroying us," the author wrote in *The Dean's December*. How unlike the twenty-first century leering over its corpse-fetishes, obsessed with murder as spectacle, is this understanding. Prime-time television serves up the hospital theater and the crime drama, parading identical bodies etherized upon a table whose unresponsive tissues are probed by knife and scalpel. Numbed by the twin analgesics of television and technology, we worry less about death than we fret about aging—living, that is. Mortality understood as the outcome of experience remains beyond the reach and attention of television and film as it does most contemporary novelists. Stories of planetary extinction we have in abundance. But death writ small in fiction (aside from the work of a few authors such as Jim Crace and Alice Sebold) is merely the tease of plot that holds distracted readers in check. Bellow's novels, on the other hand, offer serious contemplation of death as we must all finally come to it: the last day of our days, alarming in its inevitability, mundane to all but ourselves.

Mortality is to Bellow's imagination what the Big Bang is to cosmology: its prime mover and mystery, its marvel and first cause. Intellectually ambitious people ask questions that test the limits of their own thought. Just as the challenge for Einstein was to work toward an understanding of time and space, the provocation for Bellow was to make sense of the cessation of consciousness, the one event we can never know firsthand. "A man can by habit and experience, fortify himself against pain, shame, indigence," Montaigne wrote four centuries before Bellow came of age. "As for death, we can try it only once: we are all apprentices when we come to it." Like the quicksilver moment of the "now" that divides past from future time, the end of consciousness remains beyond the periphery of understanding. Death deprives us of hindsight; we lose awareness just as we begin to obtain insight into its transformative power.

Following Bellow's own lead, critics often liken the novelist's characters to the nineteenth-century types we find in Dickens and Hardy, Tolstoy and Eliot. The persistence with which Bellow's people think about their ends recalls that century's exhaustive protocols of mourning. But the rituals epitomized in Queen Victoria's forty-year funerary black compensate as much for the age's grief over the end of belief—its reluctance to let go of heaven's balm and its anxiety over the rise of technology—as for the eclipse of individual lives. Bellow's characters confront mortality with a jaunty regard far closer to Montaigne's energetic meditations than to the nineteenth-century's solemner mien. The marvelously recorded "Blue – uncertain – stumbling Buzz –" Emily Dickinson's speaker detects in "I heard a Fly buzz – when I died –" recalls the paradox Tolstoy describes in *War and Peace*, where a soldier stupefied by the chasm between stories of the war and his own participation in it has but a second to wonder how inconsequentially his life has been dispatched.

Bellow is as respectful of death as these authors, but he renders neither the drowning lung's last breath nor the heart's final contraction. His understanding is closer to that of Stanley Kunitz, who described one of his "primary thoughts through the years" as a recognition "that I am living and dying at once." Long-lived as his poet-contemporary, Bellow considers how death gives form and texture to the days that precede it. Or, again, Montaigne: "The greatnesse of the minde," the French writer insists in "Of Experience," "is not so much to drawe up and hale forward, as to know how to range, direct, and circumscribe it selfe." Fearless cartographer of the highs, lows, and embarrassments of experience, the essayist seems close kin to Bellow. Admitting our irrelevance in time and space likewise prompts the novelist to record the loopy but lovely etchings thought creates before the next wave washes away the fine tracings in the sand.

In *Ravelstein*, Bellow borrowed from the fabulous world of the Renaissance to describe the self as a "protean monster." Chick's eulogy to his mentor ("you couldn't be known thoroughly unless you found a way to communicate . . . your private metaphysics") is Bellow's as well. If the wisest man is the man who knows he knows nothing, then Bellow's job is to reveal the beautiful shapes nothing can occupy in the minds of men. His fifth and last wife joked that his temperament belonged more to the medieval shtetl than to the modern city. (And what is there to say about Bellow's women—real and fictional—except that here he was less than wise?) But his decision to represent experience writ small is an act of humility consonant with the temperament of ages rather than the Wagnerian grandiosity of our own.

Despite his contemporaries' fascination for the rigid body of logic, Bellow's abiding affection for the wispy shape of the unknowable sustained him. He found existentialism, poststructuralism, and postmodernism as arid as the Sahara without the desert's heart-stopping beauty. "The superintellectuals of the twentieth century pride themselves on their coldness and their hardness," he commented in a 1979 interview in *Quest*. "The real problem is that people now don't lead a morally expressive life." Openness to feeling and an absolute conviction in our shared human needs: these certainties left him exuberant in the small safety of the Chicago studios he rented to write in and agitated when he left them to travel home. In the crush of bus or subway (and no less than his elegant and reluctantly sympathetic character Artur Sammler), Bellow felt the impassioned hearts of fellow passengers huddled against the frigid wind off Lake Michigan or averting their heads from the dirty breeze in the tunnels disturbingly close despite the remoteness of their faces.

In Sartre and Brecht there is no such fascination with emotional life, or even regret for its lack, Bellow thought. In his books feeling breathes in vibrant prose as connected to the world as are the conceits of the metaphysical poets, Montaigne's near-contemporaries across the Channel who made a discipline of yoking unlike things together. Or the seventeenth-century wit of Andrew Marvell: like the speaker in "To His Coy Mistress," Humboldt, Herzog, and Ravelstein incite us to tear our "pleasures with rough strife / Through the iron gates of life." Even regret is charged with an antic energy that renews hope. Montaigne's confession—"there is nothing I have more continually entertained myself withal than imaginations of death, even in the most wanton time of my age"—is mirrored time and time again in the voluptuous, fevered anxieties of Bellow's central characters, whose love lives flourish not despite but to spite the unchanging dread with which they look on approaching death.

If sickness offers a vantage on health, death illuminates life, its twin, Montaigne writes. "Thou diest not because thou art sicke, but because thou art living." The trajectory of Bellow's career might be described as a gloss on this tagline. His books are exercises in thinking profoundly about how intoxicating it is to see and to hear and to breathe. From *Ravelstein*: "You came into a fully developed and articulated reality from nowhere, from nonbeing or primal oblivion. . . . In the interval of light between the darkness in which you awaited your first birth and then the darkness of death that would receive you, you must make what you could of reality." We live neither to prove the primacy of suffering nor to slog through a vale of tears. Instead, like gaudy fish weaving in and out of forests of kelp, we swim in a dapple of light.

Like Newton, whose obsession with the laws of physics did not forestall his attraction to the glister of worldly things (the scientist spent as much time tinkering with alchemy as developing experiments with gravitational attraction),

Bellow possessed a capacious imagination more sympathetic to earlier ages than the cataloguing discipline of the modern mind. There is a glorious indiscriminacy about the novels, which juxtapose the astringent pleasures of skepticism alongside lush metaphysical yearning. The journeys Bellow's quixotic wanderers make look more like the itineraries in *Tristram Shandy* or *Tom Jones* than the steady trek Frankenstein makes northward or the exhausted meandering of *The Waste Land*'s narrator alongside the refuse-strewn Thames. Bellow's voices never dishearten. They disarm with the energy of a more enchanted realm. With his puckish frame and his dreamy gaze (in photographs he looks beyond you as if toward the wild isle of Prospero's tempest-conjuring spirits), the author seems a closer relative to those who once wrote by the flickering light of candles than his twentieth-century fellows—who, safe in their centrally heated apartments, he chastised for voicing "cocktail-party" expressions of anxiety at the apocalypse. So says Bellow through Herzog, reflecting upon our taste for trauma.

No despair in this novel or elsewhere: the quality of feeling in Bellow's fictions is as vividly colored as the world our eyes reflect. The figures who people Philip Roth's books might act out their monologues on a stage devoid of props. In Bellow, by contrast, our diurnal cycles of happiness and sorrow play out in an urban world of surprising beauty. One character flushes with fear like aspen leaves twirling in a stiff wind, their bright sheen paled to sudden dullness in front of a Miracle Mile department store. Serenity steals over another like the noiseless flyover of migrating birds witnessed in the space between skyscrapers. The living and the dead, the heat of sex and the listless, disease-ridden body, the tang of red wine mixed with the rusty taste of blood: sumptuous thoughts glow inside the bodies of the middle-aged and elderly men in Bellow's novels, men startled by the ease with which a little fuel makes the soul's pilot light flare to incandescent brightness.

Ravelstein closes upon just such a blaze: "There's an early snow on the tall shrubs, the same shrubs filled with a huge flock of parrots—the ones that escaped from cages and now build their long nest sacks in the back alleys. They are feeding on the red berries. Ravelstein looks at me, laughing with pleasure and astonishment, gesturing because he can't be heard in all this bird-noise." In Dickinson's poem the failing senses blur into blue abstraction. Ravelstein refuses to yield sight or hearing. The long wavelengths of light from the scarlet berries reflect themselves in his filmed-over eye; the screech of birds knocks against his ear's unyielding tympanum. Riddled with disease, Ravelstein is vital still. Joy, a moment of sun between thunderclouds, gilds the last of life.

In earlier ages, worship remedied the severance of consciousness from the infinite. Faith bridged the distance between the visible and invisible worlds, the steadfastness of ritual a simulacrum of eternity. The obligations of daily life were small pieties that rehearsed the unknowable. Journey to market in a boat that ships water and shimmies under the weight of new passengers, and you might be reminded of the final crossing, Charon's craft pitching as shades settle to benches underneath which black water runs back and forth, a spirit balance. In past times, bed sheets billowed with wind on a clothesline like souls rising. At dawn, the silence between birdcalls conjured Genesis, the world not yet materialized out of the void. When Montaigne was writing, the prosaic could still metamorphose into the marvelous. The mineral taste of salt in your mouth recalled the wife of Lot's tears. The climbing notes of a distant flute evoked the shades beguiled by Orpheus's trespass into Hades. The ruby transparency of a pomegranate seed mirrored the longing heart of Persephone, strayed from the sunlit world of the living.

In the tradition of the American-born generation, Bellow felt the pull of ritual and refused it. But lack of observance only made the condition of reverence more necessary. "We long for enchantment, but we are too skeptical," he wrote in a 1967 essay. The glazing lights of modern civilization have swallowed the dark and locked the doors left ajar in earlier times to mystery. Art's obligation, Bellow thought, was to focus upon the dividing line between what is visible and what is not. Before our time, "artists routinely ventured farther than the eye could see," he offered in his interview with *Quest*. Baroque audiences knew that the musical intervals of Bach, Haydn, and Mozart left an echo of the celestial harmonies in the listening ear. A candle illumines half a face in a Rembrandt canvas and leaves the rest in profounder darkness. Burnished by torchlight, a painted farm's iron gate gleams gold. Rembrandt's patrons understood the virtuosity of his chiaroscuro better than we. It was not mimesis but a mnemonic this painter was after, a visual sign with which to recall the metaphysical divide behind which we continue to stand baffled, the patterning of light and shade training our eyes on the place where human brilliance ends.

Few modern artists have devoted their energies to representing things beyond measure. Bellow was one. An orthodox spiritual life was refused him by temperament and time, but he consecrated a lifetime's mornings of hard work to the moral questions prior ages recognized as religious. His interviews and essays are saturated with "revelation," "mystery," and "rapture"—the language of faith. His novels offer more direct counsel in mysticism, from the advice of the vilified Dr. Tamkin in *Seize the Day* to Charlie Citrine's characterization of religion in *Humboldt's Gift*, which "some people still speak of with respect.... It says we have ways of knowing that go beyond the organism and the senses. I've always believed that." Too skeptical to labor toward proof of God's existence, Bellow crafted sentences open to admitting the unknowable. The garrulousness of his narrators leaves a space, still, for mystery. Like Rembrandt's chiaroscuro, Bellow's writing drives toward the place where illumination gives way to shadow.

Though he laughed with relish at his own jokes, Bellow discussed his vocation with unapologetic piety. He likened the Montreal suburb where he spent his first decade to the shtetl in czarist Russia where his parents came of age and routinely described his upbringing as medieval. His childhood was shaped by his mother's desire that he grow up to become a scholar like her brothers, who looked in photographs, he recalled in 1964, as if they were living in the thirteenth century. Schooled at four in Old Testament Hebrew, Bellow was ancient, an anachronism in the twentieth century. He approached literature with the same veneration rabbinical students bring to the Talmud. Imagination furthered exploration of "the mysterious circumstance of being," he mused in a 1981 interview with Michiko Kakutani. Writing was "a spiritual activity" that allowed access to the state of absorbed openness that is the prerequisite for transcendence.

We assume that discomfort with religious culture is the outcome of modern philosophical systems and the twin revolutions of science and technology— so Bellow's quip about being a medieval man. But faith, as we are reminded with increasingly ugly frequency, has never been absent—only vigorously segregated. We shake our heads at the rise of fundamentalism, then define modernity as spiritless, refusing to notice the discrepancy in logic. Secularism is not new, but illustration of an attitude that has endured over long centuries, the distaste of intellectuals toward their cultural inferiors. The pretentiousness with which academics claim immunity from revelation and dreaming would have led Bellow to endorse both even if he had not been steeped in the study of Torah as a young child or temperamentally unable to stop yearning for a glimpse of Dante's other shore. His identification with his working-class roots constituted a form of faith, though the writer prospered in the academy. Significantly, his comfortable position at the University of Chicago did nothing to diminish his antipathy toward the people he saw as having inherited the forms and prejudices of upper-crust culture while he slogged away to create its street-smart substance. Inveterate competitiveness and a healthy narcissism no doubt added urgency to his sardonic asides, but the scorn he reserved for those he called in *Herzog* the "fashionistas" (intellectuals who shaped their ideas to suit the prejudices of the art marketplace) was genuine, motivated from the conviction that to waste even a moment of our short "interval of light" aping the despair that was de rigueur for the postwar period was the death of thinking.

Encouraging of young writers, generous with his time (a friend remembers leaving two short stories in Bellow's Chicago office on a whim and then being ushered back to the office to speak about them), and compassionate toward the foibles of his colleagues, Bellow had no patience for those who reveled in apocalypse like the petty imps of sixteenth-century frescoes to preach what he called in *Herzog* "the luxury of Destruction." "Not God is dead. That point was passed long ago." But rather, "Death is God. This generation thinks—and this is its thought of thoughts—that nothing faithful, vulnerable, fragile can be durable or have any true power." What Bellow saw as the essential soullessness of modernism and postmodernism persistently came in for rebuke. Jean-Paul Sartre, darling of the postwar media, he quoted only to dismiss. "People like Sartre understood less about left-wing politics than I had in high school," biographer James Atlas records him tossing off to Harold Kaplan. In a letter to John Berryman composed in Paris while writing *The Adventures of Augie March*, Bellow invoked the French existentialist only to subject him to characteristic comic ridicule: "Vous avez peigne ze human situation more better than J. P. Sartre avec une seule strook."

Bellow's humor entertained. More profoundly, he brandished it to refuse what Herzog calls the "bad habit" of suffering. Comedy cauterized any tendency to adopt the despondency of the victim. Invited to a banquet in Jerusalem for the twenty-fifth anniversary of the liberation of Bergen-Belsen, Atlas recalls, Bellow listened warmly to Golda Meir's feisty introduction with the memory of the Six-Day War still fresh. But Elie Wiesel's keynote lecture moved him not. While Alfred Kazin celebrated the speech in an effulgence of piety (it was a "soliloquy, a litany, a hymn, a Kaddish"), Bellow merely "looked bored." Feeling guilty for wartime misery was for Americans intellectual laziness, he thought; merely "sleep and sleep, and eat and play and fuss and sleep again," as Charlie Citrine insists in *Humboldt's Gift*. "We weren't starving," Bellow wrote there: "We weren't bugged by the police, locked up in madhouses for our ideas, arrested, deported, slave laborers sent to die in concentration camps. We were spared the holocausts and nights of terror. With our advantages we should be formulating the new basic questions for mankind."

Precisely. With a dismissive wave of the hand, the collective memory books turn into overstock. Ever the iconoclast, the Chicago writer refused to follow in the footsteps of American novelists who lingered beneath the tall smokestacks of that other world. Bellow went his own way: toward sunlight, not shadow; toward trees in leaf, not barbed wire. To settle for the smooth deceptions of big ideas, he repeatedly counseled, was to dwell in darkness rather than to delight in the "disorder" that Charlie Citrine knew "is here to stay." However baffling, life is a blessing. There are small marvels to be noticed among the general misdeeds. Step into one of his novels and feel a stream of thought slip by you like the sinuous pull of life's fast-moving current. It isn't memory we need to enshrine as holy, but life that is sacred: the sunlit world Persephone returns to each year, the land of the living Dante recalls in the ninth circle of Hell, the marriage at the close of *The Tempest*.

WONDERFUL WORLD

The Fractal Geometry of Benoit Mandelbrot

Fast on the heels of chaos theory and the butterfly effect, the whirling tendrils that compose the Mandelbrot Set cropped up on 1980s T-shirts and computer screens, record albums and magazines, posters taped to dorm room ceilings and the title sequences of sci-fi TV. A heart-shaped ink blot on the pages of textbooks, the form is an unlikely eminence. Scale its outline smaller, and it teems like the tropics. Ferns, leaves, seahorse tails, and strings of beads mass and recede in this swarming composition. Curves pirouette through the foreground and pull toward the distance. Linger on a spiral till it spins away into a branching tree. But study the math that creates these patterns and find a realm as deftly woven as the one the ancients dreamed.

On the way to the conference, as luck would have it, the car ground to a halt twenty miles north of the Hilton's chandeliered ballrooms and slow-moving escalators. Groans and a few choice expletives must have sounded inside the cabin: that afternoon, all five of its occupants were giving papers. A smattering of snow pinpricked the dashboard and vanished before more ice crystals dimpled its transparency. Benoit Mandelbrot observed the pattern, anticipating the columns that would form a fine interlacing on the cooling glass. Impossible to observe the paths of sand grains the wind dashes to ground. But if he found a way to chart the dance of these close-to-weightless discs, wouldn't he learn something new about turbulence, that coiled energy intransigent as yet to mathematical expression?

The blare of a trucker's horn bore down on the car, recalling Mandelbrot to a more prosaic if no less pressing problem. As the sixteen-wheeler rushed past, the high tone of its alarm lowered to a deeper note in obedience to the

Doppler effect. Less than a second later, the wake raised by the truck's passage slammed against the car with a thud and a cracking of windows ostensibly sealed against such atmospheric disturbance. Maybe the geometer sat stymied for a moment in the driver's seat. More likely he slid out from behind the wheel and transferred his attention from the fidgeting of his colleagues inside the car to the problem with its transmission. He was, his wife, Aliette, often supplied, an erratic and distracted driver. But World War II had turned him into a good mechanic as well as a proficient horse groomer. New York's raw winter air stole through his blazer as he opened the hood and studied the clanking, cooling machine. So what if the sky was leaden and the temperature barely in the double digits? If nothing else, war had schooled him to meteorological as well as man-made pain. Leaning over the distributor (there went his clean shirtfront), he wiped away the grease smearing the ignition points. One was pitted, presumably by a failing condenser. He extricated the part, returned to the relative warmth of the cabin, dried the condenser's metal foil, replaced the scored point with a spare he grabbed from the glove compartment, and started up the engine—which, to the astonishment of his colleagues, gasped and stammered back to life.

The whole procedure had cost them only twenty minutes discomfort, Mandelbrot reflected as the windshield wipers swept away the snow, a barely perceptible anxiety compared with wartime's quotidian dread. He had spent his teenage years hiding in plain sight in the south of France, far from Paris and his parents. Only a handful of days passed without some new terror. Would the refugee neighbor who nodded as they left the Tulle tenement at dawn turn him in before night? Would the high school colleague he chanced across in Saint-Junien accept the fake name Mandelbrot repeated slowly to cue his non-Jewish compatriot to silence? The woman he clumsily jostled on his way to the tool shop where he mended train parts: would she frown and ask to see his papers?

A gust of wind shook the car and a fresh clot of snow fell on the window. They had suffered in their separate cities, he and Léon, who his parents sent elsewhere to increase their sons' collective chance of survival. But what family had not? Alone of their circle in Warsaw, and aside from the mother and daughter who lived above their own flat, the four Mandelbrots fled to France and escaped oblivion. Detained by ailing relatives or their grand piano or their window fronting the park, the rest deferred flight. At war's end, come to Paris from the old apartment, Mrs. Braude and her daughter recounted deaths and disappearances. Horrified though she was, his mother "listened stone-faced" to their stories, Mandelbrot recalled in the memoir *The Fractalist* published two years after his death.

Now, as he drove toward the Hilton, slush slid across the glass, blurring the dreary New York landscape and encouraging the dead from that other continent to creep closer. Their familiar silhouettes clamored to be seen as the limbs of leafless trees zoomed past the rearview mirror. *There*, the perpetually pleased expression of the classmate who had strutted around Lycée Edmond Perrier repeating his parents' progressive ideas only to be hung from a lamp-post in Tulle's main square a year after Benoit and Léon fled south. *Here*, Mr. Wigdorczyk's harried face softening briefly as ten-year-old Benoit opened the door of the fourth-floor walk-up in Warsaw. *Here*, that same summer, Mrs. Goldberg's meaty arm extending in greeting from the horse cart parked by Mołodeczno's wide-gauge train track.

The Honda jolted over a pothole, jerking Mandelbrot back several decades. At ten he had clutched the side of the buggy swaying rhythmically as the old Friesian plodded across the cobbles. Snorting and snuffling, the horse pulled up short and tried to shake off its reins. Mrs. Goldberg replied by levering herself forward and coaxing the creature on, patting its rump with surprising gentleness. The little cottage Benoit slept in that summer was built into a hill wind scoured in winter. In the previous century, the remnants of Napoléon's disbanding army had stumbled past houses in this area as they retreated, Mandelbrot learned as an adult. Shrouded in snow, the hut to which Mrs. Goldberg conducted him in July's heat must have stayed snug the winter of 1812 as the French soldiers filed past its door in the -30°C temperatures, their frostbitten faces blistered black.

Dusty summers of cleared fields and deserted town squares. Winters of broken windows and lightless doorjambs. The forties were desolate, but having witnessed the maimed and the murdered, Benoit could not but thank his better fortune. Scrap iron, a metal file, poorly contrived false papers: this was Périgueux in 1943, he recalled in his memoir. Mud and manure, crude wooden clogs, a knee purpled by the falling yoke of an oxcart: these things spelled Saint-André-des-Eaux for him the following year. Villagers screaming inside a flaming church during the Christmas break at Saint-Junien. Vichy radio crackling its false cheer as Count Benoit droned the pedigree of his long-dead Lyon Derby winner at dinner. And 1944's champion? Klaus Barbie, strutting into the city in boots that barked a strike-slip-strike everyone learned to fear.

But there was still the sky, bluer than that Panzerman's eye. Also, the silvered rain that ran down the ash trees circling the estate by Pommiers-en-Forez and whose boughs, forking upward, resolved in a twiggy fretwork of slender shapes a venturesome composer might have evoked with a piccolo's climbing scale. Outside the manor where Benoit groomed horses, snow ridged the fluted sides of yellow squash piled high in a wheelbarrow. Frost crawled up the dining room window, edging the glass with a wobbly horizon of mountain peaks. Sometimes scalloped, sometimes lacy, this ice was whorled and curlicued, its ridged edge composed from countless crystals.

Did Mandelbrot explore the patterns he named "fractal" to cleave closer to nature? Or was the geometry of chaos he championed a way to think through the political disorder he survived as a young man? The meandering arcs of the Mandelbrot Set mirror the shifting contours of coastlines and clouds even as they repeat the branching conduits that bring oxygen to the lungs and blood to the tissues. "Every portion of matter may be conceived as like a garden full of plants and like a pond full of fish," Gottfried Wilhelm Liebniz announces in *The Monadology* (1714). "But every branch of a plant, every member of an animal, and every drop of fluids within it, is also such a garden or such a pond." Voltaire directed his Candide to sneer at Liebniz's rosy understanding of Earth's orchard. But surely, Mandelbrot might have reasoned from the vantage of more than two centuries' distance, the Frenchman and the German who so vehemently disagreed on metaphysics could agree upon how quickly a pond dimpled with rain restored the reflection of the branches arching over its surface once the shower stopped and how unceasingly a part of every plant inclined toward constantly shifting light. What were the petty factionalism of the academy or the small-mindedness of nation-states compared with the faith flowers hold for the sun?

And look, he told himself: the freeway had just given way to city streets. His own faith in thinking had again been rewarded: despite his inattention to the road, the car had found its way to the Hilton's tower. His colleagues climbed out of the vehicle, joking and chuckling, and then divided to their separate sessions. Mandelbrot's talk would come later. Walking through an open door upon a presentation on wave velocities already in progress, he bumped his way past knees to a front row seat—only to rise again to query the speaker before he had finished commenting upon his last slide.

The Cornell scientist behind the podium straightened his papers and shut off the projector. Coldly, he slid his eyes toward his interlocutor. Mandelbrot waited at military attention, his bulky outline conspicuous against the room's blandness, his broad shoulders rounded under his rumpled brown blazer. Tract lighting haloed the froth of hair on his nearly bald head. Speaking an accented, deliberate English that seemed at odds with his enthusiasm for argument, he outlined what was new in the paper (very little), what was distinct about its methodology (almost nothing), and what remained to be done (virtually everything). More than one in the assembled confraternity must have sighed inwardly as this scientist from the private sector plowed straight into censure. Perhaps a few shuttled their gaze from his disorderly profile to the room's featureless architecture and found the latecomer all the sloppier. Yet irresistibly, their eyes returned to the IBM interloper who had wasted no time cataloguing the weaknesses of the experiment and analysis just presented. Imagining the vulnerabilities in their own papers exposed with identical want of ceremony, was it not understandable that some steeled their hearts against his brash intelligence? As for Mandelbrot himself, who wished only to deepen his understanding: could he not sense the eyes boring into his back as he drove toward this end?

"And the exceptional variations in wave swells?" Mandelbrot raised his palms up and spread them outward like a seraphic Eastern deity, his eyes twinkling despite the oceanographer's annoyance. "What do we do with these extraordinary outliers?" He prompted, referring to the currents (not the experiment designed to measure them) with wincingly childlike curiosity. "I'm referring to the long tails. The points floating at the greatest distance from the central distribution," he supplied to aid the students in the room. There was the barest hint of drollery in his voice, as if he intended his question to speak for displaced people as well as far-flung data points. (Years later, working upon his memoir, he would be more direct, defining statistical aberrations like the outlying wave swells as examples of the "extreme inequality that is a familiar pattern in nature and in the works of humans.")

Two faculty from Paris's École Normale Supérieur exchanged glances as Mandelbrot turned toward the young people, exposing a greasy black smear on his Sears-issue shirt.

"Beer?" one hypothesized.

"Gravy or dirt?" the other quipped with a Gallic shrug.

"Stress velocities and cross-shore gradients are fine." Mandelbrot proceeded, the exchange behind him no more of an impediment than the periodic whump of air the room's heater expelled. ("Trivial," he would have told his friends in the frank shorthand with which he dismissed the uninteresting experiment, the obvious solution, and the question not worth asking.) "The large disproportions: that's where the real question is. What happens if we factor in the swells rather than dispensing with these gross variations?"

"*Ce type* could make a Brioni suit look cheap," one of the Normale men remarked as Mandelbrot gargled the "r" in "gross" in his evasive accent—part Belleville slum, part Polish ghetto, part indefinable.

The heat cycled on as the lecturer began listing surf-zone data he had collected at Nantucket Sound. Blocking out this numeric roll call, Mandelbrot watched the Sound's coastline advance and retreat in time-lapse sequence with no projector but the technology humming in his head.

The condescending physicists, the standoffish oceanographer, and the session in the Hilton are my invention. But the memories of Poland are drawn from Mandelbrot's memoir, and the breakdown, the grease-streaked shirt, and the alacrity with which he routinely discomfited scholars appear in recollections friends from physics, mathematics, music, and medicine contributed to *Fractal Geometry and Applications*, the two-volume Jubilee published to honor him during his eightieth year. Any one of the researchers who offered their reminiscences could tell you that to practice science is to find methods of measuring what you observe: leaves spinning in the wind, a skiff rocking in the wake of underwater shear turbulence, a plant sending roots around a boulder to absorb the minerals that seep into the surrounding soil. For Mandelbrot, perception accomplished without preconception was itself experiment. "To see is to believe," he insists in *The Fractal Geometry of Nature*. "Look, look, look," he repeats in *Fractals and Chaos: The Mandelbrot Set and Beyond*. Unlike rarified calculations pertinent to specific fields, the eye "is a universal tool," he recapped to art curator Nina Samuel in an interview published in *The Islands of Benoît Mandelbrot: Fractals, Chaos, and the Materiality of Thinking.*

The speed with which he could transform algebraic equation into geometric form looked like revelation, not computation. Whether you call it intuition (as his friends did), label it laziness (as his critics volunteered), or attribute it to an education disrupted by war (as he avowed in *The Fractalist*), Mandelbrot's uncanny aptitude let him sprint through proofs his high school teachers failed to finish and zip past university gates. The irregular structures he preferred examining were as different from Euclid's geometry as atonal music is from Mozartian harmony. On the eve of World War I, Henri Poincaré dismissed these shapes as a "gallery of monsters," Mandelbrot points out in his memoir. Though he grew up during the next such war, he maintained an imagination inimical to Aristotelian categorizing and a curiosity unfazed by all manner of bristling nationalisms. Hostile to intellectual constraint by temperament and time, Mandelbrot adopted the "zoo," as he fondly called the figures Poincaré disparaged, for his own. Three decades after Potsdam, this late-blooming maverick published *Les Objets Fractals: Forme, Hasard et Dimension* and gave pride of mathematical place to shapes ill-fitted for Euclid's arid planes but aptly suited to Earth's curved space. Locating complex patterns in what looked like disarray, Mandelbrot insisted fractals into acceptance by demonstrating how closely their designs followed nature's tangled forms.

Da Vinci engineered the multiple arms and legs of his Vitruvian Man to fit inside the circle Euclid defined almost two millennia before. But Mandelbrot knew intuitively that the Greek's geometry, perfect for hoisting marble into the curves of arches and domes, would not explain the organic world's wobbly, winding contours. The brambles of blackberry bushes and the cliffs of coastlines are recursive without perceptual ratio. In animals as well as plants and the landscapes that support them, serpentine vessels thrive. God may have created the world from the word, but it was Mandelbrot who would most accurately size this globe's contents. Ferns, shells, feathers, snowflakes: he "*saw* that fractals are the geometry of nature," Nathan Cohen insists in the preface to *Benoit Mandelbrot: A Life in Many Dimensions*, a collection honoring Mandelbrot after his death. "Note the absence of 'a' or 'one of.'" Mandelbrot "left no doubt of that interpretation."

Flux—not fixity—engaged him. Zephyr-like, he breathed life into equations and puffed them up into forms. He had only to conceive a shape to rotate, reflect, and resize it. Some, resenting his breezy trespassing across their disciplines, accused him of grandstanding, but Mandelbrot's facility for finding solutions was unconscious and instantaneous. Numbers cried out for notice no less than the parochial professors who scrawled them on chalkboards and typed them into textbooks. Ellipses rose into cones while vector analyses plunged into whirlpools. Peano's curve heaved up its arc into tessellated crags. Ampere's law inflated itself into doughnut-shaped toroids and polynomials rushed to repeat their sequences in patterns that expanded in Mandelbrot's head faster than fireworks rush their contrails through the dark skies above fields and fairgrounds. "Bottomless wonders spring from simple rules . . . repeated without end," he pronounced these strangely beautiful shapes in a TED talk a few months before his death, relying once again on the unadorned language that grated on so many scholar specialists.

"Can the projector be turned back on?" Mandelbrot interrupted the oceanographer droning out data.

Mutely, the Cornell scientist returned to his PowerPoint.

"*There.*" Mandelbrot pointed to a black point vibrating on the matte white screen. "*And there*"—he raised his arm to gesture toward a dot swimming far from the myriad clustered in a brightly lit quadrant. "*And again, here,*" he continued, waving his hand rapidly through the air as if to gather in three specks so widely scattered they might have been mistaken for dust on the projector lens. "What would happen," asked this man whose thought could jump lightning-quick from geometry to physics and branch out into music and art, "if we came up with an equation that accounted for these wanderers?" He smiled at the rest, narrowing his eyes as if he were staring at the sun rather than the lesser lights of the Normale physicists. "If we could establish one, we could connect the orbits of stars with the eddies in whirlpools."

His challenge was genial, but turbulence coursed from the first row to the back seat. A few, lulled by the hum of the ventilation system or the oceanographer's monotone, straightened their spines against the hard metal backs of the chairs. A trio argued, a larger mass in the middle of the room revised, and two students on one end of a back row gesticulated as if to amplify. Four people in turn scrawled elaborate equations on the poster propped by the podium. A phalanx of statisticians from Harvard's Earth and Planetary Sciences leaned forward in their seats as Mandelbrot lined out one numerical sequence and scribbled a corrective. Nodding vigorously, a marine geologist whose curly black hair was sprinkled with silver scrawled a note on the pad of paper at his elbow. "But—" began an oceanographer from Oxford without being heard. "What about the—" he interjected a second time, then slumped before the verbal onslaught with tired, pouchy eyes. A chemical oceanographer from Scripps took Mandelbrot's cue and proposed a clarification that veered sharply away from the general line. Like a cloud of electrons, fine brown hair frizzed about her face. Mandelbrot listened to her suggestion, pondered a second, and smiled. The Normale professors raised their eyebrows into supercilious half-moons. "Galaxies" to their graduate students, Peter Jones recalls in *Benoit Mandelbrot: A Life in Many Dimensions*, they were accustomed to being acclaimed, not ignored.

People filed in for the next session, bringing the easygoing fracas to a close. The impromptu discussants dispersed, leaving a few who carried on without glancing up at the newcomers. No, he had not expected to arrive at the Hilton looking like a mechanic, Mandelbrot answered two biologists with whom he was arguing about cardiac vascular structure. The car he was driving had stopped en route, he explained cheerily, pronouncing the last two syllables in that French the Normale scholars found so peculiar. But why wait hours for a tow if you could fix the problem in a few minutes? He added, raising his palms up in the quizzical gesture characteristic of him.

Did he brush shoulders with his French detractors before he left the room? If so, rebutting their frosty smiles, he might have assured them that his long-ago decision to withdraw from their institution after a single day's matriculation jumpstarted his career and catalyzed his theory of roughness. *Ah, yes*, they would have nodded with tight faces. *Fractals*. Pretty patterns. Elegant, even, the equation. But what, more precisely, could his computations do?

Others had let this question hang in the air at conferences in economics, in linguistics, and in astrophysics. More would repeat the query before Mandelbrot, blinked at by the academy, was finally ushered into its fold. Yale awarded him a Sterling Professorship in Mathematics in 1975, but he would wait another twelve years to be tenured. Given the glacially slow recognition of his brilliance, the verbal dart thrown by the Normale scholar must have sailed past him with no more ceremony than the buzz of a fly. An iconoclast only loosely rooted in his own era, Mandelbrot repeatedly refused to follow a conventional career trajectory in order to maintain what he calls in *The Fractalist* (and always with a romantic flourish) his "Keplerian dream." Prodigious insights like the one Mandelbrot worked toward possess a reach so uncommon they are rarely acknowledged in the discoverer's lifetime. How marvelous, then, that he enjoyed an annus mirabilis in his fifties after describing the repeating forms mathematician Adrien Douady honored as the Mandelbrot Sett. The celebrity status he attained after was merely icing on the cake.

Under the gray walls of the Hilton's conference room, a group of students awaited his attention, the turquoise and canary-yellow reproduction of his Set swirling conspicuously on the cover of *The Fractal Geometry of Nature* they clutched under their arms or pressed close to their chests. Before detaching himself from the Normale elite to sign books, the geometer might have told these physicists that he had chosen to attend college at the Polytechnique, their foremost rival. Would he have recalled for them the trip back to Paris from the farm where he had labored with his head down to protect his counterfeit papers? Unlikely, since this posture was one he steadily refused to reprise. He might have announced that the Bourbaki cult's dry-as-dust approach then favored by Normale mathematicians had prompted him to reject their institution. In those days the Normale mathematicians were austere as monks, adamant in refusing the aid of images in proof and equation, and entirely unable to anticipate the irregular shapes Mandelbrot was himself investigating. The Polytechnique had given him room to flourish, he might have insisted. There, no arid theoreticians had turned their backs on the amorphous and the strange. He was fortunate the Normale had let him go without a murmur, since choosing to leave and being turned away had produced equal possibilities.

What could fractals *do*? What couldn't they do would have been the better question, Mandelbrot might have murmured inwardly. Biologists use fractals to understand how insects distribute themselves in trees, cardiologists exploit them to identify the heart-rate patterns that produce life-threatening arrhythmias, and cosmologists manipulate them to develop equations about the contours of space-time. He had named them after the verb *frangere* to honor the Latin of his long past youth, he explained in his TED talk. But "fractus" is a "break" that also unifies. Juxtapose a photograph of cigarette smoke and one of an interstellar gas cloud thousands of light-years across, he proposes in *The Fractal Geometry of Nature*, and look in vain for their difference. Armed with a conviction that bordered on evangelicalism and an energy that verged on the prophetic, he insisted to all who would listen (and many who would not) that his zoo of shapes knit natural phenomena into an arrangement as artful as the design the Old Testament attributes to the deity. The resistance to changes in scale that provides fractals their self-similarity would give him—the one who named them—leeway to generalize across experiment and hopscotch from field to field.

He began his career by fine-tuning linguist George Zipf's law of word frequency distribution, jumped to geography to formulate an argument about the fractal nature of coastlines, then swerved into economics to propose a direly accurate model for stock market crashes. "What a joy to quote the Bible as a pure scientific reference!" he exclaims in *The Fractalist*, having gleefully labeled the 1929 and 1987 market crashes the "Noah effect" and named the sustained dependency of price shifts on prior conditions after Joseph, the analyst of dreams who had so accurately predicted lean and fat years for Pharaoh. "In mathematical terms," economist Richard Hudson translates in *Benoit Mandelbrot: A Life in Many Dimensions* for those of us fazed by the lexicon of his field, "Mandelbrot was saying that the guideposts that all prior financial theory" depended on "were in fact illusory."

The fractalist's own shifts from city to city and job to job seem no less meandering than the ragged contours his math revealed. In exposing hidden relationships between what seem to be entirely isolated mechanisms, the succession of experiments he conducted appear themselves to possess a fractal character. As a wave distributes its energy across the water, so the Zipf-Mandelbrot law explains the abundance of species ecologists study and ear-pleasing metrics musicians explore. Twigs maintain the proportions their parent branches establish, while the endless curves contained within continents mirror the limitless twisting of lung tissue packed within the chest. In turn, both rock outcroppings and alveolar arcs gesture toward the infinite variety of price shifts in the stock market, Mandelbrot argued. If the never-ending budding and dividing of the Mandelbrot Set restructures perception, so the manifold applications of fractal theory remodel thought. And yet the equation that creates the ark that shelters this immense range of terrestrial and celestial objects is as dazzlingly simple as Einstein's own. Take "z," multiply it by itself, and add "c" to obtain the branching, whirling contours of the black blot Mandelbrot derived through the laborious calculations of IBM's first behemoth computers.

Showy, the Normale academics would have sniffed had they heard the researcher from IBM crowing about the shape he called the most complicated in mathematics. *Grandiose*, they might have added had they known he claimed likeness with Einstein, that supernova of scientists. Yet if da Vinci's Vitruvian Man glorified humanity as driver of the world's wheels, Mandelbrot's more irregular shapes reduce us to minute mechanisms in a vast natural drama. We can sweeten this fall, as did he, by recognizing the rhythms of our hearts, the pulses of our neurons and the cycling of oxygen through our lungs as no less fractal in structure than the gasses that stream across space.

From fracture to fractal and war to wonder is not, after all, so great a leap. In 1944, as Mandelbrot rubbed down gentlemen's horses, himself skinny as a rail and terrified of capture, could he envision the marvelous traces of order in the mess? The most astonishing fact of his life is not that he survived war's disaster but that he refused bitterness over its damage. His mother's forsaken dental degree and his father's forgotten aptitude for invention, his own relocations across countries and removals to habitations ever shabbier and draftier, the pepper of gunfire outside windows beneath which he slept and the whispered recitations of torture he intercepted for those caught with false papers: such traumas might have stopped a man of lesser energy. How could the young Mandelbrot not feel as "solo, perdido, and abandonado" as Puccini's Manon, whose aria he so admired? To counter such difficulty, he lost himself filing metal shards into the smooth join of spare parts to coax dynamited trains back into motion. After work, he watched water boil over rocks knowing that the froth leaking away between boulders offered illustration of the moon's forcing of tides. In the end, who better to approach turbulence (that writhing monster of modern mechanics) than a man grown up in war's whirlwind? Accepting suffering as the catalyst for his mathematical second sight, Mandelbrot converted the liability of his disrupted education into the gift of fiercely independent thinking.

Did his heart beat a little faster when he rose to contradict the oceanographer in that hotel room full of scholars irritated by his question? Did a hint of the estrangement that was his constant companion during wartime trouble his mind? If so, was it also possible that as the seconds ticked by the geometrical shapes blooming in his inner eye were overtaken by the figures that had once crouched in crawl spaces and hurried past soldiers and shuffled past guards? Might he then have had to will himself to remain standing? At twenty, he recalls in his memoir, he thought himself "a strong-willed person with clearly defined tastes." At eighty he insisted on the blessing of knowing precisely who he was even as "successive bureaucracies" remained endlessly perplexed. Was he "ungentlemanly," as a rival scientist called him in a slur an April 1990 issue of the *Scientific American* repeated a bit too quickly? Certainly. But while Mandelbrot was raised in Belleville and only tardily made a French citizen, he remained as impervious to scholarly factions as to political divides. For decades—through the reshuffling of the postwar period and the long years of useful but uncelebrated work at IBM—he brought his arguments to academia only to see them scoffed at, sniffed over, and ignored. After each rejection, a lonely figure under the light, he rose to speak his next idea into appearance.

CODA

When I first read Grace Paley in my twenties, I could not hear her characters speak. Had I chanced upon the clamorous street the narrator of "The Loudest Voice" looks back upon, I would have had no difficulty settling down to read amid its familiar cacophony. The grade schoolers who scrub construction paper turkeys off streaky windows to make space for "new shapes" in red and green paper would have returned me to schoolyard chatter just as quickly. After all, I was barely a decade removed from cutting out snowflakes and reindeer myself.

But ever the dutiful student, I turned the title page of Paley's *The Little Disturbances of Man* and ran smack into the middle-aged woman whose voice sets "Goodbye and Good Luck" going in the ringing tones of an old alarm clock. "I was popular in certain circles, says Aunt Rose. I wasn't no thinner then, only more stationary in the flesh. In time to come, Lillie, don't be surprised—change is a fact of God. From this no one is excused." Rose was solid: I could not get around her. There was a staunchness in her emphatic double negative I also could not escape. Assuming that glee in midlife was a contradiction in terms, however, I registered none of the jauntiness in her verbal delivery. Nor, preoccupied with establishing gloom, could I spot the rapacious desire for life that offsets defeat. Now that I am Rose's age, I can see that Paley's core metaphysics offered echoes of wartime dauntlessness to grown-up readers. But when I first read her, I was just venturing out in the world and thought the staying power in this fiction about as thrilling as a limpet clutching a rock.

Suffering: this was hard to miss in her work. While still a teenager, Paley's father served prison terms in Russia and Siberia. At an equally young age, readers of *Just As I Thought* learn, the writer's mother was exiled. The rest of the terrors—revolutions, pogroms, and the murders of relatives—these two kept to themselves, convinced the past was "a swamp of despair" in which their children "could only sink." Or maybe, Paley continues, rolling a clutch of unvarnished nouns into a catalogue at breakneck speed, they were just "too busy" with "English, school, work, family, life" to offer more before their "story ended."

With the same shock of hours upended, the narrator of "Goodbye and Good Luck" spies the "rotten handwriting of time" on her mother's cheeks and "across her forehead" and runs their implications together in a jumble of hurried fragments: "Back and forth—a child could read—it said old, old old." At twentysomething, I understood Paley's repeated sonority here as expletive rather than honorarium. Naturally, I whizzed past descriptions of Rose's too too solid flesh and missed the spirit underneath. The alloy of grief and humor that girds and girdles her and a host of other Paley characters was an amalgam too mixed for me to interpret. And then I still believed in plot, a literary stratagem the fictional daughter in "A Conversation with My Father" dismisses as "the absolute line between two points." "Everyone," she goes on in this story, "real or invented, deserves the open destiny of life." Bent on reading for discernably happy endings, willing to accept tragic conclusions where happiness, I assumed, could not possibly find purchase, I did not so much follow along this story and others as skitter over the ellipses, circles, and tangents Paley improvises upon the taut lines of her sentences.

Things changed, just as Aunt Rose promised they would.

I got a little older—old enough to want to forestall endings rather than hurtle pell-mell toward them. I had a daughter. Finding my mother's blush in my child's laughing face, I realized there was more to living and writing than adhering to the lockstep march of the present. As I typed out compound, complex sentences and slogged toward the close of my dissertation, I began to obtain an inkling of what it might take to create the high-wire syntax of dives and somersaults Paley's narrators execute with such finesse upon each story's tightrope. Then, when I was a graduate student in my thirties balancing Zoë on my hip, Paley read in Berkeley. As her compact figure sang out a story in her Bronx accent, I caught the blend of rue and relish in her characters' accents. All at once, people and places resolved into as clear a focus as if I had been handed the aural equivalent of opera glasses.

Why hadn't I heard the music of her sentences earlier? Maybe, having fled Boston when I went to college, I had closed my ears to the acerbic inflections that were second nature to me. Maybe I was trying too hard to look out for my glamorous future to recognize the "ordinary place and terrible time" Paley names in "Other Mothers" and that almost all of her characters accept as their bailiwick. Or maybe I had not yet developed enough respect for language to see that it could not just provide escape from my then present circumstances but offer a way to root me more firmly in the actual. Listening to Paley, I realized that virtuosic twists and turns of phrase rather than pedestrian sequencing of events drive her stories. "The sound of the story comes first," I read much later in a 1992 interview she sat for the *Paris Review*: "A story can begin with someone speaking. 'I was popular in certain circles,' for example; an aunt of mine said that, and it hung around in my head for a long time. Eventually I wrote a story, 'Goodbye and Good Luck,' that began with that line, though it had nothing to do with my aunt."

In "The Value of Not Understanding Everything," a piece that could speak as easily for the unknowns Einstein, Rothko, Bellow, and Feynman look toward, Paley identifies the mystery that spurs her writing in terms of what she cannot properly hear rather than what she does not easily see. "My family spoke Russian, but the street spoke Yiddish. There were families of experience I was cut off from. You know, it seemed to me that an entire world was whispering in the other room. In order to get to the core of it all, I used all those sibilant clues. I made fiction."

Now that I am in my late fifties, I have no difficulty detecting grins alongside the audible sighs in Paley's sentences. Nowhere does that mingling of sounds speak to me more directly than in "Mother," a piece as virtuosic as it is brief. Exposition, development, recapitulation, coda: in ten paragraphs, three of which are single sentences, Paley plays upon time, offering readers the entire sonata structure of human relations. We hear variations on the theme of marriage: ("They sat in comfortable leather chairs. They were listening to Mozart. They looked at one another amazed. It seemed to them that they'd just come over on the boat"), notes of longing between couples ("She said to him, Talk to me a little. We don't talk so much anymore") and between parent and child, ("I heard a song: 'Oh, I Long to See My Mother in the Doorway.' By God! I said, I understand that song. I have often longed to see my mother in the doorway"), dissonances ("I'm tired, he said. Can't you see?"), recapitulations

("I wish I could see her in the doorway of the living room"), and melodies that reverberate into silence ("Then she died.").

To call this piece a gesture sketch would get at its Mozartian lightness of finish. But as I listened to its spare sentences climb upward and plummet downward and hang steady in air, they seemed to me to render not so much the silhouettes of lives in contact as the dense substance of loneliness in the midst of shared experience. I have taught this story to hundreds of students. And yet, as I linger this time through on the distances between intimates it represents so ably, it is my own mother I see—a woman who frequently played second fiddle to my father's louder and seemingly more dynamic music, a person I frequently railed against for not hearing me, a mother who continues, even today, to stand in the doorway waiting and smiling at me, as I in turn wait for her and the return of her eighty-four-year-old memory. Stubborn? Yes. Staunch? Absolutely. Stoic? Always. And so rather than rush to the end, let me go back (if only rhetorically) to our respective beginnings and open a window or door in your own memory; and ask you in turn, as I have asked my mother so many times and have finally perhaps learned to demand of myself: *just listen.*

APPENDIX

The following chronology provides a partial set of works discussed in this book as correlated with historical events in Europe between 1933 and 1945. Neither set of dates is exhaustive.

1933:   Hitler appointed chancellor of Germany

1938:   Kristallnacht; Austria seized

1939:   invasion of Czechoslovakia; invasion of Poland; Britain and France declare war; Einstein writes a letter to Roosevelt warning him about the effects of weapons of mass destruction

1940:   invasion of Denmark and Norway; Blitzkrieg against Holland and Belgium; Dunkirk; Italy enters the war as an Axis power; France signs armistice with Germany; Battle of Britain

1941:   Yugoslavia attacked; Russia attacked despite 1939 nonaggression pact; Pearl Harbor; Britain and the United States declare war on Japan

1942:   Allies fight against Rommel in North Africa; Battle of Stalingrad

1943:   Axis powers defeated in North Africa; Italy surrenders

1944:   siege of Leningrad ends; D-Day; Paris liberated; Battle of the Bulge

1945:   Roosevelt dies, and Truman succeeds him; German forces surrender; Germany divided into four military zones directed by France, Britain, the USSR, and the United States; atomic bombs dropped on Hiroshima and Nagasaki; Japan surrenders

Einstein, theory of special relativity, 1905
Einstein, theory of general relativity, 1915
Chagall, *Birthday*, 1915
Chagall, *The Promenade*, 1917
Chagall, *Over the Village*, 1914–18

Chagall, *The Rabbi*, 1922

Gershwin, world premiere of *Rhapsody in Blue*, 1924

Chagall, *Jew with Torah*, 1925

Gershwin, world premiere of *An American in Paris*, 1928

Gershwin, "I Got Rhythm," 1930

Gershwin, world premiere of *Porgy and Bess*, 1935

Chagall, *White Crucifixion*; Copland, world premiere of *Billy the Kid*;
   George and Ira Gershwin, "Love Is Here to Stay," 1938

Chagall, *The Burning Village*, 1940

Copland, world premiere of *Rodeo*, 1942

Manhattan Project, 1942–46

Copland, world premiere of *Appalachian Spring*; Bellow, *Dangling Man*;
   Rothko, *Aubade* and *Slow Swirl at the Edge of the Sea*, 1944

Alfred Einstein, *Mozart: His Character, His Work*, 1945

Rothko, *Yellow, Cherry, Orange*; Bellow, *The Victim*; Primo Levi, *Se questo
   è un uomo*, 1947

Rothko, *Violet, Black, Orange, Yellow on White and Red*, 1949

Copland, *Music and Imagination*, 1952

Rothko, *Rust and Blue*; Bellow, *The Adventures of Augie March*, 1953

Rothko, *Earth and Green*, 1955

Bellow, *Seize the Day*, 1956

Rothko, Seagram Murals, 1958–59

Bellow, *Henderson the Rain King*; Paley, *The Little Disturbances of Man*, 1959

Rothko, Rothko Chapel canvases, 1964–67

Bellow, *Herzog*, 1964

Mandelbrot, "How Long Is the Coast of Britain?," 1967

Bellow, *Mr. Sammler's Planet*, 1970

Primo Levi, *The Periodic Table*; Mandelbrot, *Les Objets fractals: Forme,
   hasard et dimension*; Bellow, *Humboldt's Gift*; Paley, *Enormous Changes
   at the Last Minute*, 1975

Mandelbrot, *The Fractal Geometry of Nature*, 1982

Paley, *Later the Same Day*, 1985

Bellow, *Ravelstein*, 2000

FOR FURTHER READING

Introduction

Almost seventy-five years after their initial publication, Aaron Copland's Norton lectures, published as *Music and Imagination* (Cambridge, Mass.: Harvard University Press, 1952), still make for engaging reading alongside his younger friend and fellow composer Leonard Bernstein's *The Unanswered Question: Six Talks at Harvard* (Cambridge, Mass.: Harvard University Press, 1976).

Richard Feynman published a number of books on physics directed at the inquisitive nonscientist. The three talks he delivered at the University of Washington in 1963 as part of the Jesse and John Danz Lecture Series became the core of the 1998 project his children published ten years after their father's death: Michelle and Carl Feynman, *The Meaning of It All: Thoughts of a Citizen-Scientist* (New York: Perseus Books, 1998). *Six Easy Pieces: Essentials of Physics Explained by Its Most Brilliant Teacher* (Cambridge, Mass.: Perseus Books, 1994), a collection of six of the most accessible chapters from Feynman's 1963 book *Lectures on Physics* (Boston: Addison-Wesley), which was prepared for publication by Robert B. Leighton and Matthew L. Sands, offers more food for thought. Physicist Leonard Mlodinow's portrait, *Feynman's Rainbow: A Search for Beauty in Physics and in Life* (New York: Warner Books, 2003), provides readers with a series of lively, wide-ranging exchanges between the two men.

Iconoclasm con Brio: A Reminiscence

André Aciman's beautiful memoir *Out of Egypt* (New York: Riverhead Books, 1994) offers readers a striking portrait of a particular Sephardic Jewish family as well as a sensuous evocation of Alexandria prior to Nasser.

Dislocation and Invention: A Fugue

Alfred Einstein's *Mozart: His Character, His Work* (New York: Oxford University Press, 1945) remains a standard of Mozart studies. Maynard Solomon, *Mozart: A Life* (New York: HarperCollins, 1995) offers insight into the life as well as the work of this composer. Two shorter and eminently readable studies are Peter Gay's *Mozart: A Life* (New York: Viking Adult, 1999) and Paul Johnson's *Mozart: A Life* (New York: Viking Adult, 2013).

Antecedent: The Energy of Exodus

The Jewish Study Bible (Oxford: Oxford University Press, 2004), ed. Adele Berlin, Mark Zvi Brettler, and Michael Fishbane, provides thoroughgoing notes. For the first five books of the Bible, Robert Alter's *The Five Books of Moses* offers extensive commentary. His *The Hebrew Bible: A Translation with Commentary* (New York: W. W. Norton, 2018) weighs in at 3,500 pages but provides extensive historical context as well as brilliant commentary.

Stargazing in the Atomic Age

Brian Greene's *The Elegant Universe* (New York: W. W. Norton, 1999) and *The Fabric of the Cosmos: Space, Time, and the Texture of Reality* (New York: Knopf, 2003) provide an excellent if densely written pair of volumes introducing twentieth- and twenty-first-century developments in theoretical physics and string theory. Simon Singh's lively and lucent *Big Bang: The Origin of the Universe* (New York: 4th Estate, 2004) offers an excellent introduction to cosmology. Caleb Scharf's *The Copernicus Complex: Our Cosmic Significance in a Universe of Planets and Probabilities* (New York: Scientific American/FSG, 2014) provides a meditation at once down-to-earth and poetic on how we can understand scientific developments in cosmology while keeping in mind our particular location far from the center of our own galaxy.

Feynman's two memoirs—*"Surely You're Joking, Mr. Feynman!": Adventures of a Curious Character"*(with Ralph Leighton; New York: W. W. Norton, 1985) and *"What Do You Care What Other People Think?": Further Adventures of a Curious Character* (with Ralph Leighton; New York: W. W. Norton, 1988)—are inimitable Feynman: down-to-earth and deftly pitched to a general audience. James Gleick's *Genius: The Life and Science of Richard Feynman* (New York: Vintage, 1993) provides an expansive and beautifully written portrait of this physicist.

There are as many hundreds of excellent meditations and biographies of Einstein as there are of Mozart. I found Corey S. Powell's *God in the Equation: How Einstein Transformed Religion* (New York: Free Press, 2002) useful as a study of Einstein's science over and against his penchant for mystery. Peter Galison's engaging *Einstein's Clocks, Poincare's Maps: Empires of Time* (New York: W. W. Norton, 2003) historicizes time and in so doing provides thoughtful and often overlooked context on the scientist's discovery of relativity. Einstein's *The World as I See It* (Secaucus, N.J.: Citadel Press, 1979) should be required reading for anyone who wishes to learn more about Einstein's attitudes on ethics as well as science. I found *Albert Einstein, The Human Side: New Glimpses from His Archives*, selected and edited by Helen Dukas and Banesh Hoffman (Princeton, N.J.: Princeton University Press, 1979), equally indispensable as a window into his thought.

Kai Bird and Martin J. Sherwin's *American Prometheus: The Triumph and Tragedy of J. Robert Oppenheimer* (New York: Knopf, 2005) is the first full-scale biography of this American scientist and makes for thoughtful reading.

Leaving Russia: The Soulful Modernism of Chagall and Rothko

I relied heavily on Orlando Figes's twin studies of Russian history and culture—*A People's Tragedy: The Russian Revolution 1891–1924* (New York: Penguin, 1996) and *Natasha's Dance: A Cultural History of Russia* (New York: Picador, 2002)—which provide thoroughgoing introductions to Chagall's and Rothko's birthplaces. *Hope against Hope*, trans. Max Hayward (1970; repr., New York: Modern Library, 1999), the first of two memoirs by Nadezhda Mandelstam detailing life with husband and poet Osip Mandelstam, who was arrested in 1934 and who died in 1938 as one of many victims of Stalin's purges, speaks directly and urgently to political tensions during the first decades of the Soviet period.

Stanley Kunitz's brilliant translations of Akhmatova can be found in *The Collected Poems* (New York: W. W. Norton, 2000) as well as in *Passing Through: The Later Poems, New and Selected* (New York: W. W. Norton, 1995).

James E. B. Breslin's magisterial *Mark Rothko: A Biography* (Chicago: University of Chicago Press, 1993) remains the first study of the painter and the best place for readers to start who wish to learn more about this painter's life and work. Christopher Rothko's *Mark Rothko: From the Inside Out* (New Haven, Conn.: Yale University Press, 2015) offers a thoughtful reexamination of his father's work.

Along with its beautiful color plates, Jacob Baal-Teshuva's commentary on Chagall's work in *Marc Chagall: 1887–1985* (Los Angeles: Taschen, 2003) is a thorough and engaging study. Chagall's lilting autobiography *My Life* (New York: Da Capo, 1960) is as indispensable as it is engrossing. Bella Chagall's *Burning Lights* (1946; repr., New York: Schocken, 1962) is equally readable and includes thirty-six of the artist's line drawings.

Listening to Gershwin

For general background on twentieth-century music, Alex Ross's lively *The Rest Is Noise: Listening to the Twentieth Century* (New York: FSG, 2007) is very helpful. Readers wishing to concentrate more fully on music theory writ large as well as the long history of musical scales (pentatonic and heptatonic) can learn a great deal from Stuart Isacoff's fascinating *Temperament: How Music Became a Battleground for the Great Minds of Western Civilization* (New York: Vintage, 2001).

Copland is an excellent guide to his own music. *Copland on Music* (New York: W. W. Norton, 1963) offers a representative sample of his writings. His two-volume autobiography, written in conjunction with Vivian Perlis—*Copland: 1900–1942* (New York: St. Martin's Press, 1984) and *Copland Since 1943* (New York: St. Martin's Press, 1989)—provides an excellent record of his career. Howard Pollack does justice to his life and work in *Aaron Copland: The Life and Work of an Uncommon Man* (Urbana: University of Illinois Press, 1999).

I found Pollack's excellent and definitive study *George Gershwin: His Life and Work* (Berkeley: University of California Press, 2006) immensely useful. For sources contemporary with this composer, Isaac Goldberg's *George Gershwin: A Study in American Music* (1931; repr., New York: Frederick Ungar Publishing, 1958) cannot be equaled. Merle Armitage's *George Gershwin, Man and Legend* (1958; repr., New York: Da Capo, 1995) is excellent, and Robert Wyatt and John Andrew Johnson's *The George Gershwin Reader* (New York: Oxford University Press, 2004) showcases a broad range of perspectives on Gershwin.

Though it is fiction, Henry Roth's *Call It Sleep* (1934) offers a brilliant study of Russian Jewish immigration in the early twentieth century even as it provides a somber lyric counterpoint to Gershwin's musical effervescence.

Questions of Transport

Giovanni Boccaccio's *Life of Dante*, trans. J. G. Nichols (circa 1350–55; repr., London: Hesperus Press, 2002), was written less than thirty years after Dante's death and so carries the distinction not only of its author but of the fact that it provides a window into Dante and the politics of his time during his own period. I relied as well on Barbara Reynolds's *Dante: The Poet, the Political Thinker, the Man* (London: Shoemaker Hoard Press, 2006), Erich Auerbach's *Dante: Poet of the Secular World* (New York: NYRB, 2001), and R. W. B. Lewis's *Dante* (London: Weidenfeld and Nicolson, 2001).

For readers willing to take the time to work their way through it, Carole Angier's *The Double Bond: Primo Levi, A Biography* (New York: FSG, 2002) provides a fulsome look at Levi. Levi's beautiful memoir *The Periodic Table*, trans. Raymond Rosenthal (1975; repr., New York: Schocken Books, 1984), provides the most acute insights into his early years, his work as a chemist, and the aftermath of Auschwitz and closes with a particularly elegant and life-affirming essay, "Carbon." A collection of his unpublished stories translated by Ann Goldstein and Alessandra Bastaglia as *A Tranquil Star: Primo Levi, Unpublished Stories* (New York: W. W. Norton, 2007) offers oblique but fascinating perspectives on his life and world.

For general philosophical background I found Susan Neiman's *Evil in Modern Thought: An Alternative History of Philosophy* (Princeton, N.J.: Princeton University Press, 2002) very readable and extraordinarily compelling.

In Praise of Bellow

James Atlas's *Bellow, A Biography* (New York: Random House, 2000) has now largely been supplanted by Zachary Leader's capacious and commanding approach to the writer in two volumes *The Life of Saul Bellow: To Fame and Fortune, 1915–1964* (New York: Vintage, 2015) and *The Life of Saul Bellow: Love and Strive, 1965–2005* (New York: Vintage, 2018). Son Gregory Bellow provides a candid and direct appraisal of his father in *Saul Bellow's Heart: A Son's Memoir* (New York: Bloomsbury, USA, 2013). Edward Mendelson's elegant essay on Bellow in *Moral Agents: Eight Twentieth-Century American Writers* (New York: NYRB, 2015) follows Bellow's own lead in its yoking of aesthetics and ethics.

Wonderful World: The Fractal Geometry of Benoit Mandelbrot

First and foremost, I relied upon Mandelbrot's exuberant memoir *The Fractalist: Memoir of a Scientific Maverick* (New York: Pantheon, 2012). Mandelbrot's introduction to his textbook *The Fractal Geometry of Nature* (1977; repr., New York: W. H. Freeman, 1983) provides an intriguing, accessible overview of his mathematics. *The Islands of Benoît Mandelbrot: Fractals, Chaos, and the Materiality of Thinking*, ed. Nina Samuels (New York: Bard Graduate Center, 2012), considers links between images and numerals in Mandelbrot's thought. The 2004 Jubilee publication *Fractal Geometry and Applications: A Jubilee of Benoit Mandelbrot*, ed. Michel L. Lapidus and Machiel van Frankenhuijsen (Providence, R.I.: American Mathematical Society), provides more technical field-specific studies of applications of Mandelbrot's fractal geometry.

James Gleick's *Chaos: Making a New Science* (1987; repr., New York: Penguin, 2008) offers readers a stellar introduction to chaos theory more largely.

Coda

To my mind, Paley on Paley is irresistible. I found *Just As I Thought* (New York: FSG, 1998) as direct and down-to-earth as it is brilliant. Readers can find her three volumes of stories collected in *The Collected Stories* (New York: FSG, 1994).

GEORGIA REVIEW BOOKS

What Persists: Selected Essays on Poetry from The Georgia Review, *1988–2014*, by Judith Kitchen

Conscientious Thinking: Making Sense in an Age of Idiot Savants, by David Bosworth

Stargazing in the Atomic Age: Essays, by Anne Goldman